A Little Bird Told Me So

Birds in Mythology and History

A Little Bird Told Me So

Birds in Mythology and History

Eleanor H. Stickney

Rutledge Books, Inc. Danbury, CT

Copyright© 1997 by Eleanor H. Stickney

ALL RIGHTS RESERVED
Rutledge Books, Inc.
107 Mill Plain Road, Danbury, CT 06811
1-800-278-8533

Manufactured in the United States of America

Cataloging in Publication Data
Stickney, Eleanor H.
  A little bird told me so
  ISBN 1-887750-67-3

  1. Birds — Greece. 2. Birds — Mythology
598.2   97-68319

To my beloved husband, Albert Stickney, Jr.
who "is not for the Birds."

Dodo

About the Author

Eleanor "Ellie" Stickney became interested in birds as a child and went on to major in Ornithology in college. At the same time she worked in the Bird Department of the American Museum of Natural History in New York City where they published her paper on wintering shorebirds on various Pacific Islands in their "Novitates" series. For 45 years she has been licensed by the United States Fish and Wildlife Service to trap, net, band and release wild birds. She spent nearly 30 years as Collections Manager of the Bird Department at Yale University's Peabody Museum of Natural History where another paper of hers was published in their "Postilla" series. She also spent five years organizing and running the "Peabody Museum Associates" and was its first president.

Ellie has come from a long line of bird people. Her great, great uncle, George Newbold Lawrence of New York (1805-1895) was one of the founders of the American Ornithologist's Union and Honorary member of the Linnaean Society of New York. He wrote 121 scientific papers on birds, had one genus and 20 bird species named after him. He described 323 new species from the Caribbean, New Mexico, Central and South America. He also worked with Baird and Cassin on the famous Pacific Railroad Report and was a friend of John James Audubon.

A bit closer to Ellie was her grandfather, Harold Herrick, who married Lawrence's niece. He was one of the founders of the Linnaean Society. A businessman and amateur Ornithologist, he described a new Warbler at Chatham, New Jersey in April 1874. Eventually, it was called a hybrid between the Golden-winged and Blue-winged Warblers. Of these the Brewster's is the dominant and the much rarer Lawrence's is the recessive hybrid of that crossing.

Retired now, Ellie has been a frequent public speaker, much sought after for the lecture that was the inspiration for this book. *A Little Bird Told Me So* represents the culmination of years of dedicated love and research. Ellie and her husband now reside in Essex, Connecticut.

Special Thanks to John Maisano

John Maisano has worked in fields as various as architecture and theater design. He has received and executed commissions for both oils and acrylics. His cartoon drawings are a particular favorite at Yale's Peabody Museum where he has worked for the last seven years creating paintings and exhibit murals in oil and airbrush paints, sign-making and designing exhibits—not to mention birthday and holiday decorations—such as ten foot high dinosaurs for the Museum lobby. He also has received commissions from a number of scientists. In his spare time, John Maisano plays the guitar and continues his education in the arts.

Foreword

Ellie Stickney is one person whom birds have been telling things to all her life. I have known a lot of bird enthusiasts, from erudite scientists to Roger Tory Peterson and people who are simply gaga about a particular kind of bird. None of them, I would say, gets more joy out of an interest in birds, or more radiates a contagious enthusiasm than Ellie. It has been my good fortune to know her and be her friend from my very first year in college where her office at the Peabody Museum of Natural History and her home in Guilford were always open to me.

All these years Ellie has been adding to her knowledge about birds and collecting esoterica and folklore about different species. Thank goodness she has distilled all that energy, effort, knowledge and enthusiasm in this little book. If ever you have had a flicker of interest in birds you will surely find something to intrigue you herein. And no matter how encyclopedic you may be on matters ornithological you will find choice tidbits new to you, because I don't believe there is anyone else who could have put together this book.

So enjoy your excursion from Lascaux to Lewis and Clark in what may be thought of as a yellow pages of birds and folklore. You have the best of all guides, short of a chorus of birds telling you these things themselves...and even they might fall short of conveying the sheer fun of it that only Ellie-the one and only-brings to it all.

Thomas E. Lovejoy
Counselor to the Secretary
Smithsonian Institution

Introduction

A Little Bird Told Me So is based on the belief that birds had their own language and could give information to people. You will see this as you go through this collection of facts, fantasies, fallacies and folklore. This tells us much about the lives, habits and religions of the past and is a picturesque part of all national literature. Birds have featured in the imaginative life of man since earliest times. They have appeared as part of his superstitious and religious life. This is understandable because of the variable nature of birds. Some have gaudy plumages, others dull feathers, some have lovely voices which others lack, some can imitate or mimic, some make noises at night, while others have semihuman-like characteristics, and they all appear and disappear. Above all, they fly into the sky where the gods live, which is unattainable to man.

The earliest pictorial record that we have of a bird comes from the walls of the Lascaux Cave in France dating from the Stone Age. There, next to a Bison who has killed a man, sits a bird ready to take flight. This may be the first instance of the soul being represented as a winged creature. Early Egyptian burial pictures showed a bird flying from the body of the deceased. They are credited with the idea that a bird is the symbol of the human soul. In early Christian paintings, birds were frequently pictured as flying out of the mouths of dying saints. Angels, martyrs and saints were often portrayed with assorted types of wings.

Birds are constantly in contact with humans and can be easily observed. They seem to do the same things year after year and do not change their habits. They appear to be more active at dawn and at dusk, and in the spring and fall. Birds are masters of the sky and a link between heaven and earth. They build their nests, lay their eggs and raise their young on the earth. In the sky, however, they are associated with the gods, sun, moon, stars, wind, rain and other forms of the weather. The ancient Persians used their coming and goings as the basis for their first calendar. Even Aristophanes, in the 5th century B.C., said that birds lived before the Gods were born and ruled over nations. The Cock was the King of the Persians, the Kite ruled over Greece and the Cuckoo took care of Egypt and Phoenicia!

Their use in religious superstitions were especially rife up to and through the Middle Ages. They carried so many overtones and undertones, as the Middle Ages were the greatest time for misinterpretation of natural history. The early Christian centuries were anything but a period of scientific research. People read "The Bestiary," written by Christian teachers who were interested in natural history and, wanting to explain the Scriptures, in so doing allegorized them. St. Augustine went as far as to say that it did not matter if an animal or bird did or did not exist. What mattered was what it was symbolically. Art helped foster folklore as did the signs of the zodiac, the fancy embroidered Dragons of China, the Sphinx and murals of the Nile, the science of heraldry and its use of symbols. Bird song and bird flight gave augurs, seers and shamans and the like, news of the will of the gods. All over the world you find many variations on the same theme by people trying to explain avian activities as they affected their lives. Here are a few examples: how birds were changed from one color to another; how they got their feathers; the parts they played in the Great Flood and the origin of the world; how the time of planting and harvesting was governed by the arrival or departure of certain birds and their ability to forecast the weather; the direction from which the first song is heard in the spring; and all sorts of illnesses and their cures that were attributed to certain birds. The Native Americans had a special interest in the colors of their feathers. They related this to compass directions and their meanings varied from tribe to tribe. This was also the case in their use of certain feathers in their rituals.

Migration myths included many birds. According to several Native American tribes, eons ago, the birds played ball with the North Wind. Those who won stayed on all year, while the losers fled south. In 1703, "a man of piety and great learning" wrote (based on Jeremiah 8:7) "An essay towards the probable solution to this question. Whence come the Stork, the Turtle (Dove), the Crane and the Swallow, when they know and observe the appointed time of their coming?" His sage solution to the problem was that they went to the moon in sixty days at great speed unless they could find another place to go! Christopher Columbus changed the course of his ships to follow a flight of birds and avoid a mutiny, and so made his famous landing. Mark Catesby in the 17th century said that the reason there were so few birds in the New World was because they had a hard time getting there after the Flood!

Weather has always been of primary concern to people throughout the ages. A nice example of this is Richard Inwards' poem of 1853, published in "Weatherlore."

> "If the birds be silent, expect thunder
> If fowls roll in the sand,
> Rain is at hand.
> If the wild geese gang out at sea
> Good weather there surely will be.
> If Larks fly high and sing long
> Expect fine weather.
> When Man-of-War hawks fly
> High it is a sign of a clear sky
> When they fly low, prepare for a blow."

The word "bird" stems from the Anglo-Saxon word "brid," meaning the young of all birds from Sparrows to Eagles, while the adults were called fowls. These terms were used from approximately 1150 to 1500 A.D. when both were termed "byrd" and finally "bird."

Birds have given rise to several sayings. In 1500 in England, a gang of criminals were called "birds of a feather." It now has a more general use! "Bird brain" means that you are governed by instinct and not by thinking. A "bird's-eye view" means looking down from on high like a bird and getting the whole picture. Other common expressions are "a bird in the hand is worth more than two in the nest or the bush," "better an egg today than a hen tomorrow" and "better a Sparrow in the hand than a Stork on the roof." All of these mean that you are better off with what you have than looking for greener pastures!

As you start reading the "truths" of yesteryear, you may pick up some new information about birds. Some of these birds will be familiar and others new to you, but they all have held mysteries, secrets and beliefs to people all over the world. Remember, "a little bird told you so," or, as Aristophanes said in 414 B.C., "no one knows except perhaps some bird."

Albatross *Diomedea*

The thirteen species of these highly pelagic seabirds with tube noses and a wing span of six to eleven feet are usually lumped into one or two species by mariners. The best known and the biggest is the four foot tall Wandering Albatross, *Diomedea exulans*, with their eleven foot wing span. They are famous for their awkward courtship displays of dancing, bowing, sweeping and clicking their beaks. The word albatross came originally from the Arabic and then the Portuguese word "alcatraz" meaning large seabird. They have several local names such as "Mollymawk, Mollyhawk and Molly" from the Dutch "mallemok" meaning stupid gull. The Japanese called them "Kakadori" or fool birds. Our word goon comes from their slang name of gooney or goney. Their scientific name *Diomedea* comes from Diomedas, A Greek hero of the Trojan War who was said to be buried on one of the Adriatic Islands named after him, the Diomedae.

These birds have always been a part of the legends and lore of the sea. The Albatross was made famous by Samuel Taylor Coleridge's poem "The Rime of the Ancient Mariner," which was based on the belief that if you killed one, bad luck would come your way. These birds were thought to be the spirits of seamen swept overboard in gales, so were considered to be harbingers of wind, fog and rain. However, many sailors killed them to make tobacco pouches out of their webbed feet and pipe stems from their long wing bones.

On many Pacific Islands, they were thought to be messengers from the gods. They were said to sleep in the air, as their flight was so motionless, and they laid their eggs on a raft-type floating nest. An Easter Island deity is adorned with the beak of an Albatross.

In 1909, three thousand Laysan Albatross *Diomedea immutabilis* were killed for their plumage causing President Theodore Roosevelt to declare Laysan Island a wildlife reservation in order to save the remaining birds. More recently, at Midway Island Airfield, these birds became a menace to high speed jets. One bird sucked into a jet could explode the plane. To stop this problem, the birds were transplanted to other islands but they always came back to their original home. Finally, the dunes near the runways were bulldozed. This eliminated the updrafts that the birds formerly used to ride into the paths of the planes. This time it worked!

Anhinga *Anhinga anhinga 34"*

These dark colored birds of fresh water ponds, streams and lakes are usually found singly from the southeast United States to Argentina. They look similar to Cormorants but have a much thinner and longer neck, and a pointed tail. This bird gets its name from the language of the Amazonian Tupi Indians who called it "Water-turkey." In parts of the United States, we call it "Water-turkey" as well as "Snake-bird" as it appears to swim with only its head above water. Another name given to it is "Darter" as it spears its fish with a rapier-like bill.

Ani *Crotophaga 14"*

These are glossy, shiny blackbirds with a long tail and an odd bill, the top of which is high, thin and curved. Several females lay their eggs in layers in a communal nest and all the adults take turns in incubating and raising the young. There could be as many as twenty-six eggs in one nest. This is a far cry from their relatives, the European Cuckoos, who lay their eggs in other birds' nests. Anis are known to the people of the West Indies as "Black-witch, Savanna blackbird, Jumbie-bird, Topi or Mel kobo." They have been accused of several mispractices in their lives. In reality, these three species are harmless and beneficial birds of the southern United States, Central and South America.

Auk, Great *Pinguinus impennis 30"*

This name is from the Scandinavian word meaning seabird. When Jacques Cartier landed on the islands of the North Atlantic in 1534, he encountered thousands and thousands of what were called Penguins because of their black and white plumage and their "pin-wing." Though they may look alike, Auks and Penguins are not related nor do they live in the same areas. Cartier filled three boats with them for fuel and food. Other fishermen did the same for years until they became scarce. On the Island of Eldey, off Iceland in 1844, the last two birds and their single egg were taken. The Great Auk had become an extinct species. Having no use of their "pin-wings," they had trouble walking on land but no problems in the water. In ancient days, it was said that if a man's gait was unsteady and not straight, he was called "drunk as an Auk."

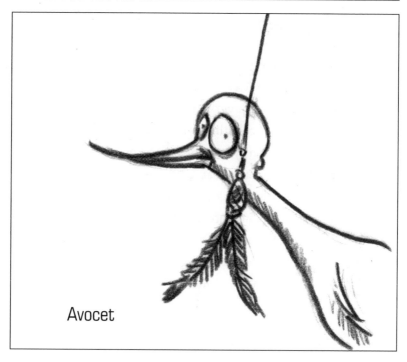

Avocet

Avocet *Recurvirostra avocetta 17"*

Their scientific name means bent bill. They are sometimes called "Awl-bird or Cobbler's-awl" because of the likeness of their bill to that tool and because it resembles the scoop used by boatmen to throw water on their sails. These birds are unmistakable with their long, slender upturned bills, black and white plumage and long gray legs. To eat, they sweep their bills from side to side. In Norfolk and Suffolk, England, puddings were made out of their eggs and their feathers were used for artificial flies by fishermen. The Dutch called them "Kluut" for their melodious sound of "kluiwit." There are four species of Avocets in the world.

Barbet, Crimson-throated
Megalaima rubricapilla 6"

B arbets are a large family that range from Africa to India to the Philippines, Borneo, Sumatra, as well as from Costa Rica to Brazil and Paraguay. All the members of their family are noisy and feisty with loud strident voices. Because of this feature, they have earned the names of "Coppersmith, Blacksmith and Tinkerbird." Even more descriptive is the name "Brain-fever-bird" as they are constantly repeating their monosyllabic clang-ings that eventually "get" to people. They are gaudy and chunky with bristles around the bill — hence their name Barbet. This is the bird that was the "Coppersmith" of Rudyard Kipling's "Rikki-Tikki-Tavi" whose metallic "took" told of the news that Rikki had killed the Cobras, Nag and Nagaima. The call of this Southeastern Asian relative of the Woodpecker has a hollow res-onant noise that can be repeated eighty times a minute!

Bee-eater *Merops 8-14"*

T hese relatives of the Kingfishers are found in the tropical and temperate areas of the Old World. They are slim, sleek birds with down-curved bills who get insects in the air. They are very colorful and mainly green. They have patches of red, blue or yel-low on the head or rump and most have long central tail feathers.

Aelainus said that they flew backwards and when they got old, they never left their children's nest which was a six foot hole! How could they? Aristotle said that the young took care of feed-ing their ancient parents. He had this fable mixed up with that of the Hoopoe!

Bellbirds *Procnais 11"*

These Cotingas are tropical and get their name from the Amazonian Indians' for the White Bellbird which meant washed white. The male of these fruit-eating birds utter extremely loud metallic calls from well separated areas in the tropical forests while perched on special display branches. They also boast of an extensible wattle springing from the base of the bill. You can not miss this noise when you visit most any big zoo.

Birds of Paradise *6-18"*

There are 43 species of these highly exotic, colored birds. In the 16th and 17th centuries, traders from Portugal called them "Manucodpiata." This is a corruption of the Malay phrase "manug dewata" meaning the birds of god. In the Middle Ages, they were thought to feed "on the dews of heaven and the odor of flowers." They had no feet or legs so that they could never rest on land. The reason for this was the fact that the Portuguese traders removed their legs and feet before shipping them to Europe. This was to show off just their beautiful plumages. It was also thought that they came in flocks to the ripe nutmeg trees and the odor intoxicated them so they fell to the ground where the ants ate off their legs and feet. This was used as an example to those who strayed from the path of temperance!

In New Guinea, nearby islands and northern Australia where they occur, their feathers were used for headdresses for chiefs. These would be mixed with Cockatoo feathers and shells. This mixture was a merging of yellow, pink, scarlet, violet, blue, orange, black and white. The shimmering blue breast of the Bluebird of Paradise and the gold tail spread of the Greater Bird of Paradise were the most spectacular and desired. Feathers from the males of a lot of species were used in commercial trading until it was banned in 1924 but illicit hunting still occurs. The first known ones to reach Europe were sent to the King of Spain by the Ruler of Batjan in the Molluca Islands and carried on Magellan's ship Victoria in 1522. Three hundred and fifty years later Alfred Russell Wallace came in the 1850s to the same place. There, he discovered the Standard-winged Bird of Paradise which carries his name *Semioptera wallaceii*. This small thrush-sized brown bird has a shiny green gorget at its throat which he spreads when displaying. He also has two six inch white pennant feathers extending out from his wings that he erects into a V over his back when courting. Wallace took two live Birds of Paradise back to England in 1862. These were the first of the family to reach Europe alive. In the eighteen eighties over fifty thousand skins were shipped to Paris, the feather headquarters. This became the favorite prowling ground for ornithologists looking for new species!

Bittern *12-30"*

These twelve relatives of the Herons inhabit reedy marshes and are colored like their surroundings. They use their camouflage colors in times of danger by freezing their bodies, heads, neck and bill upwards like a stick. They get the name Bittern from the Latin "butire" because of their cries.

There are many fanciful tales about these birds. From Pliny 27-79 A.D. comes "lowing like an ox," made by inserting its bill in a reed or in the ground and making a booming sound. Turner in England went as far as to say "so far as I can remember it is nearly the color of a Pheasant and the back is smeared with mud, it utters braying noises like those of an ass." Added to this, they were said to have the property of emitting a light from their breasts that was equal to a torch illuminating the water so they could find their prey. Their cries are described as croaking, booming, braying or belching. This gave them the local names of thunder-pumper and stake-driver. An Aztec legend said that if the Bittern sang a lot then rain would come down and therefore there would be more aquatic life and fish. However, if it sang only every third day, the rain would be light and the fish few. In Europe, if you put a bittern's claw in your buttonhole, fastened with a ribbon, it would bring you good luck. Its long toes were used as toothpicks and often mounted in silver, the middle toe being the best. In England in the 14th century, fines were levied for taking its eggs. Its flesh was considered less fishy than that of the Heron. In the 1542 food report it said, "A Bittern is not so hard digestion as a Heron." Maybe that is why it was a favorite food of Henry the Eighth.

Here is the answer to sleeplessness? These birds are great eel eaters so after a meal they rub their heads with powder down from their breasts. They leave it on for a spell and then comb it out, scratching hard with the serrated nail of the middle toe. When it is clean again, it waterproofs itself with oil from its preen gland. So if you are in need of sleep quickly grind up a Bittern's bill and take the powder!

Blackbirds *New World*

There are ninety-four species in this family who range from six to twenty-one inches in size and are not all black. They are called "Icterids" and include many unfamiliar as well as familiar birds. These include the Blackbirds, Orioles, Cowbirds, Grackles, Meadowlarks and the Bobolink. The European Blackbird, Grackle and Oriole are not members of this family.

Blackbird, Red-winged
Agelaius phoenicus 8 3/4"

From Louisiana comes the story of how this bird got its red and yellow epaulets. It seems that a man set fire to a marsh and a little bird flew up to object. This made the man very angry so he picked up a shell and threw it at the bird, wounding its wings and making them bleed, hence those colors.

Blackbird, Rusty _Euphagus carolinus 9"_

In Labrador, people kept these birds in cages as pets. The owners seem to enjoy their cunning and mimicry in spite of the fact they are far from beautiful. They are rusty only in the fall. In summer they look like a small, short-tailed Grackle with a yellow eye.

Blackbird, Yellow-headed
Xanthocephalus xanthocephalus 10"

This is a marsh loving bird of Canada and the Western parts of the States and really has a bright yellow head. The Pueblo said that their yellow plumage was the color of pollen and that was a welcome sign. When the birds returned in the spring, it meant summer was just ahead.

Bluebird, Eastern _Sialia sialis 6-7"_

The Pilgrims called this member of the Thrush family "Blue Robin" after the "Robin Redbreast" that they had left behind in the Old World. These blue-backed, pink-breasted birds have large eyes and slender bills. Their young resemble Robins in being speckled. They like nest boxes but there is competition for

9

them from Starlings, House Sparrows and Tree Swallows. They became the bird of happiness and the bringer of good luck thanks to Maeterlinck's "The Bluebird." Blue is a symbolic color. The arrival of the Bluebird in spring means that summer will soon be coming and that is always good news. "The blues" mean sadness. The Cherokee said that blue was the color of the North and that meant trouble. However, "true blue" means loyalty and faithfulness, so take your choice.

Bluebird, Mountain *Sialia curroides 7 1/4"*

The male of this western bird has a sky-blue back and paler breast and prefers open areas over 5000 feet altitude. There is a Native American legend of how this bird got its blue colors. Originally, it was a dull grey bird but because it was so gentle, it was allowed to bathe in a certain lake of blue water that had no inlet or outlet. The bird bathed for five mornings and on the fourth emerged naked. On the fifth day, it had acquired a coat of bright blue feathers. Another myth is that after the Flood, the chief God, Tirawa, sent the Bluebird to look around. When it returned with news, it was told that it would be the chief of all the birds once people came back to earth again. To commemorate this act, the Bluebird was placed on their ceremonial pipes. It was sacred to some tribes as its blue color in their beliefs was the color of the south and the herald of the rising sun. To others, its color stood for the north and so the bird was not popular. It was however, the symbol of the changing seasons when it came and went on its migrations. The Hopi used their feathers for the winter solstice ceremonial prayer-sticks to indicate that the bird would soon be arriving. Bluebirds flying around a hogan (house) at sunrise meant good luck.

Bluebird, Western *Sialia mexicana 7"*

These western birds were said to be a rain bird as their chattering cry was supposed to bring on the summer rains. As they were seen only in the summer in some areas, their spring and fall migrations were most important to some tribes.

Bowerbirds *9-15"*

A unique family of nineteen birds that are related to Birds of Paradise and live in the same areas. They can be divided into four groups: the no-builders, the stage builders, the maypole builders and the avenue builders. It is hard to believe that the male makes these areas just as a female enticer and a mating place. She then goes elsewhere to make a simple nest.

The no-builders are two species of Catbird (no relation to the American Catbirds) known for their cat-like calls. The stage builders put fresh leaves on a cleared space and replace the dead ones. The maypole builders make their poles by piling sticks and twigs horizontally at the base of a small tree four to six feet high. The male then goes to a nearby tree and builds a pyramid around it, and arches over the space between with vines and sticks like a roof. Then he decorates the walls and ground with mosses, ferns, flowers, small shells and bright berries. He even replaces the dead ones with new material. The avenue builders use smaller areas, only partially roofed but highly specialized. He makes a mat of twigs and sticks several inches thick and well trodden. In the center, he erects two parallel walls of upright twigs that are firmly entwined. He may or may not roof it but it must be wide enough for him to walk through. Next, he decorates this playhouse with pebbles, bones, shells, leaves and flowers. To paint he

Bowerbird

uses a sort of dauber with which to decorate it. To paint, the Regent Bowerbird *Seiculus chrysocephalus* uses a wad of green leaves while the Satin Bowerbird *Ptiilonorhynchus violaceus* uses a wad of bark. The paint is of charcoal and other pigments mixed with their saliva, and comes out a sort of blue-green color. Some artisans!

Brant *Branta bernicla 25"*

This small black-necked Goose has black underparts, back and head, with a white rear. This Mallard-sized bird gets its name from the Latin for dark color. They are called Brent in Europe. The Passamaquaddy have a story of how one of their heroes had to become one of these birds while on a heroic journey.

Bulbul

In ancient Arabic this name was used for a small bird and Omar Khayyam used it widely in his poetry. They are mainly an Old World family of Africa and Southeast Asia. They number 119 species and vary in size from 6 to 11 inches. They have a patch of vaneless feathers on the nape of the neck. Their bills are slender and slightly down-curved with some being notched and others hooked. They are mostly dull gray, brown, dull yellow or black with patches of yellow, red or white on the head and undertail. Some are crested and they all are cheerful with pleasant songs.

Painted Bunting *Passerina ciris 5 1/2"*

To some Native Americans, this beautifully colored male bird of red, yellow and blue represented nadir. That is part of the heavens under our feet, being the opposite of zenith. Its color gives rise to its other name of "Nonpariel."

Snow Bunting *Plectrophenax nivalis 6 3/4"*

To the people of the far north, where this bird is circumpolar, it is most welcome. This black and white member of the Sparrow family cheerily twitters as it feeds on the coldest of days. It is considered a symbol of hope and the promise of better days ahead.

Canary *Serinus canaria 5"*

This bird was named for the Canary Islands from where these caged birds were imported to Europe in the 16th century. They are supposed to be very sensitive to odors. In bygone days,

Canary

miners took them into coal mines as they were more alert to gases than humans. If a bird got drowsy or fell unconscious, it was time to leave the mine. The Chinese in the Western World kept them in illicit opium dens. If they got sick, the owners felt that the smell must be going outside and they would get caught: a sort of litmus paper test. If a stray cat killed your Canary, you would have two years of bad luck. If it sang in the dark, it was about to die. On the plus side, if you put a leaf of sage in its nest, then it would lay eggs. If you wanted peace then you put a Canary and a Goldfinch together in your cage!

Caracara

There are nine species of these Birds of Prey that are found mainly in South America. However, the **Crested Caracara** *Polyborus plancus* 20-25" is the national bird of Mexico and is also found in South-central Florida, Southeast Texas and Southwest Arizona but not in great numbers. They are long-legged, long-necked dark birds with a black crest and red on their naked faces. They like open areas and spend a lot of time on the ground. The Tupi Indians gave them their name and the Inca esteemed them for their pugnacious nature and their black and white plumage which they displayed on their imperial regalia. These birds are very aggressive and top the list among the New World scavengers.

Cardinal, Northern
Cardinalis cardinalis 8 3/4"

Their name originated from the red robes of the Cardinals of the Roman Catholic Church. They used to be a popular caged bird and known in Europe as the "Virginia Nightingale" though a New World species where they are loved as the "Red bird". As for being a great songster, they really just repeat a few notes. To some Native Americans, they represented the South and the West because of their color. The male is red all over with a black face, red crest and heavy red bill. The female is a buffy brown with red tinges on her crest, wings and tail but has the dark face and red bill. They both "sing" most of the year. Their Southern range is moving northward and into Canada, and they have been successfully introduced into Bermuda. They are the leading state bird. Illinois, Indiana, Kentucky, North

Carolina, Ohio, Virginia and West Virginia have adopted them, and do not forget the baseball team of the St. Louis Cardinals.

Cassowary *Casuarius 50-65"*

There are three species and several subspecies of these large, powerful ratites that inhabit Australia, New Guinea and adjacent islands. They have short, stout legs, heavy bodies, no tail feathers, rudimentary wings and a big boney helmet on their foreheads, and live in the forests. The New Guinea Hill People put a premium value on their bare primary shaft feathers as they used them as a nose septum and in head ornaments. They had to go to the coast to pick up the young birds and take them back inland to raise them. These birds are very bad-tempered and attack with leaping feet that have powerful sharp claws. Adults can be very dangerous but apparently the natives felt it worth the risk of maybe getting killed!

Catbird, Gray *Dumetella carolinensis 8 3/4"*

This gray bird with a black cap and russet under tail feathers is in the Mockingbird family. The name Catbird comes from its song that sounds like the mewing of a cat. They are found all over the United States except for the very southwestern part. Alexander Wilson, the famed ornithologist-painter, blasted the theory that the Black Snake had the power to charm a Catbird. He observed that the Catbird was usually the assailant and usually successful. There is a common expression "to be in the Catbird seat."

Chaffinch *Fringilla coelebs 6"*

This Old World seedeater is a common bird throughout Europe and gets its English name from "the finch of the chaff." This refers to the straw of the manger of the Nativity. Linnaeus used the scientific name *coelebs*, meaning celibate, because the two sexes stay apart in flocks except in the breeding period. In 1758, it was the first bird of many to be given the name of *Fringilla* by Linneaus.

Chat, Yellow-breasted *Icteria virens 7 1/2"*

It is the largest member of the Warbler family with a very yellow breast, dark back, long tail and thick bill. It has a loud voice and can mimic. The Pueblo said that it represented the north and was said to carry pollen. Therefore, its feathers could be used on prayer-sticks.

Chickadee
Parus 5"

These little birds are in the Titmouse family. This name is based on the word "tit" meaning anything small and "mose" a general name for small dull colored birds. You cannot miss their black cap and bib and white cheeks. They very kindly sing their name. You can find them all over the northern United States, southern Canada and Alaska. This busy bird is easily lured to bird feeders and especially to sunflower seeds.

In Labrador, you never hurt one because of this legend. The Chickadee was the keeper of time, the recorder of moons. These were recorded by making notches in its bill. The natives also kept a notch stick, but in any argument, they went to the boss, the

Chickadee. September had one notch, October had two, November had three, December had four, January had five and February had six. Then they started all over again. It must have been hard for the Chickadee to enjoy his seeds with all those notches in his mouth!

Chicken/Cock/Fowl

They were domesticated from the Red Jungle Fowl *Gallus gallus* of Southeast Asia around 2500 B.C. They were known in China by 1400 B.C. and in the Mediterranean area about two centuries later, brought there by Phoenician ships. They were among the first birds to be domesticated. They were likewise a chief

Cock

source of food, sacrifice and myths. Aristotle spoke of them as "The Persian Bird." The Greek leaders in charge of the Battle of Marathon in 490 B.C. ordered a cockfight exhibition for the soldiers before they went into that battle. The men were so inspired that they beat the Persians. Abraham Lincoln got the nickname of "Honest Abe" because he was such a fair judge at cockfights.

The Romans found the will of the Gods in the behavior of the chicken and had an official called the "Pullarius" who looked after the flocks. These birds were easy to watch and were on hand when needed. The sacred "Pulli" accompanied the armies and navies, and, if they would not eat, then there would be no battle. Fighting cocks were rubbed with garlic before fights and in India they were given garlic when wounded or fainting. It was forbidden to eat them as their hens were good egg layers. Barnyard cocks were said to have a stone in their gizzards called "alectoris" and its possessor got strength, courage, money, success with women and even invisibility!

Cocks were also used as timekeepers. The Hebrews had four periods of the night. Cock crowing was the third and the most welcome as all the apparitions of the night would soon be leaving. The Romans had the night divided into periods of one and a half hours each. The second was when these birds started to crow, followed by the next when they ceased crowing, and then finally dawn. Cock decoys have been placed in church steeples as a watch-bird and as a symbol of the second Advent.

Probably the most famous bird noise in history was the crowing of the cock after Peter's denials on the eve of the Crucifixion. History tells of Admiral Rodney's famous cock, who on April 12, 1782, while perched on the poop of the flagship, clapped his wings at every broadside that was poured into the French ship "Ville de Paris." In the Revolutionary War, there were two famous cocks who made history. They were said to belong to a Captain Caldwell of Delaware who said that they were the offspring of an "Old Blue Hen." The soldiers claimed that they were just as good fighters as those cocks so Delaware became the "Blue Hen State." Its people were then known as the "Blue Hen's Chickens." These birds are also mixed up in black magic, voodoo and folk medicine. Place a chicken on a snakebite and the poison will leave. If you were feeling badly, you would hang a chicken around your neck so it flew into your chest. When it cheeped or flapped its wings, the bird was absorbing your problem and soon you would be cured. Pliny said that the bile of a white cock or the dung of a red one would cure cataracts. White hens were in disfavor for breeding as they were easy prey due to their color so were used to hatch peacock and duck eggs. They were also used in sacrifices to nymphs and to Aphrodite and were sacred to Zeus. Their noise went unnoticed but not so the crowing of the red one. It was warning of something. The crowing of the black hen meant that evil was leaving so it was offered to the Goddess of the Night.

The Chicken/Cock/Fowl had many attributes. The Aztec often substituted a cock for a human in sacrifices. Lions were said to go into retreat on hearing them crow. If you boiled one up and applied it to your body, it would scare away lions and panthers. In China, the white cock denoted purity of heart so brides and grooms ate white sugar cocks at their weddings. They were a symbol of fertility to the Slavs and Hungarians. The bridegroom carried one or its image in his wedding procession. Black cocks were offered by the Druids to evil spirits, but to the French they were therapeutic. They claimed by taking three drinks of water from the skull of one, speech would be restored to a maiden struck dumb by the fairies! People thought that epilepsy could be cured by burning one with the nails and hair of a patient. Cock ale was a general remedy for ill health. Chicken broth, if taken by mouth, cured a number of problems. They included paralyzed and palsied limbs, diseases of the joints, liver and kidney disorders, bladder infections, indigestion, headaches, asthma, flatulence, loss of appetite and of course prolonged fevers.

To the ancients, if a cock showed any signs of homosexual tendencies, it meant disaster and so was instantly burned alive. It was sacred to Apollo and the bird of the sun. However, in China it was the bird of the moon.

As these birds were fed and protected by man, they did not need any intelligence so became known as "stupid." Young fowl are very timid and run to the wing of the hen at the slightest cause for alarm, hence the word "chicken-hearted." The word "cocktail" supposedly originated in the Revolutionary War as a mixed liquor drink served in a glass with a feather from a cock's tail in it. There was a theory that long-shaped eggs were supposed to be males and were better eating! The Bantam Cock was symbolic of pluckiness and priggishness, while the Cock stood for vigilance and overbearing insolence. As a matter of prudence, on hearing a cock crow or an ass bray, you had better spit. Beware however, when the cock stops crowing: then Judgment Day is at hand!

Chicken, Prairie *Tympanuchus 17"*

These Grouse are heavily barred brown birds with dark elongated neck feathers. In courtship, the male erects his neck feathers and inflates the orange-red sacs on his neck, emitting a loud booming noise. This is accompanied by a spectacular dance. The cock runs a few feet, stamping his feet. Then he pivots in circles and spreads his tail like a fan. He then snaps it together with a loud click and starts to boom. All this to attract a mate. Several males doing this at the same time can create quite a racket. Their courtship dance so fascinated the Dakota tribes that they fashioned their mating dance after that of these birds. These birds used to roam over the Central United States but their range is now very limited because of the advance of "civilization." Their former lands have now disappeared.

Chough *Pyrrhocorax 15"*

This name is pronounced "chuff." The two species are members of the Crow family. They have glossy black feathers, red legs and a turned down bill. In one species it is red and in the other it is yellow. They are noted for their acrobatic stunts in the air, and are found in Europe and the British Isles. They are protected in Cornwall as the soul of King Arthur was supposed to have migrated into one of these birds. Even devils could change themselves into Choughs or so it was said. The red-billed species is said to love fire and could tell a husband of his wife's infidelity. Their black color was said to foretell rain, famine and even sterility. Quite some birds!

Chuck-will's Widow
Caprimulgus carolinensis 12"

It is the largest of the Nightjars, with mottled buffy brown feathers that blend into its surroundings. This is a trait of the entire family. This bird is nocturnal, an insect eater with a small but wide bill plus small legs and feet. It has a habit of repeating its call over and over again. It has been regarded with superstitious awe whenever it is seen or heard outside of its normal southern range in eastern North America. An early American writer in New England, where it is rare, was quoted as saying: "I recollect once to have known a whole village in New England in terror and amazement at hearing one sing a strange song at the edge of a swamp. The superstitious members of the village considered it a prediction of some evil that was to befall a widow of the parish, but there was a diversity of opinion as to who the Chuck-will's Widow might be."

Cock of the Rock *Rupicola 12"*

There are two species of this tropical Cotinga in South America. In one species the male is red in color and in the other it is orange, and both are solitary and arboreal. Both females have warm brown feathers. What makes these birds so odd is that their helmet-like crest conceals their bills. The males gather at "leks" and each clears a court on the forest floor to display his plumage and attract a mate. After mating, she does all the work as she is left alone to make a nest and raise their young.

Condor, Andean *Vultur gryphus 52"*

Like its rare relative the California Condor, it has a wing spread of ten feet and weighs twenty to twenty-five pounds. It is bare-headed like the rest of the American Vultures. This probably has to do with their carrion eating habits as their feathers would be a problem! They all have great eyesight and are known to live for a long time in captivity. This South American bird had a hard time being recognized as a real bird. Early travelers told of its great size and ferocity so no one believed that it really existed. It wasn't until 1791 that it became a reality. A specimen finally arrived at the British Museum and then it became a real bird.

It is represented as from Peru where at Machu Picchu there is a Temple of the Condor. To the Inca they were a symbol of strength. Since the first century this bird was used in symbolic or mystical ways until the Spanish Conquest when it lost out to the Hawk. However, it was placed on the coats of arms of Bolivia, Chile, Colombia, Ecuador and Peru.

Condor, California
Vultur californianus 45-55"

This silent bird is a lingering relic of the Pleistocene Age that included the Woolly Mammoth and the Mastodon. The word Condor comes from the Peruvian word "cuntur," their name for Condors. This bird is about twice the size of the Turkey Vulture, with adults having a red/orange bald head while the young have dusky heads. Their plumage is blackish with the adults having white linings to the wings which the young lack.

This bird was often confused with the legendary Thunderbird as it soared beyond a spear's throw or sling shot or arrow. It was said to be superior to all others as the maker of wind, the creator of storms, and the source of thunder and lightning. It was even believed that when the bird was angry it caused thunder and lightning so it would be able to capture a whole whale and carry it back to its home on a mountain peak. Some of the West Coast tribes said that it was the Great Abductor as it carried off maidens and even captured the wives of other birds!

The Central Miwok of California used the skin of this bird in some of their dances. The main dancer would put his legs through the holes where the bird's legs used to be and then laced up the skin over his body with the dancer's head projecting out. He had some red painted on his face, a few feathers in his hair and the Condor's wings tied to his arms. This left the birds' tail to drag on the ground. The Condor ceremony was a very important date to them as they killed this bird-god as a substitute for their own deaths. They felt reborn again when they saw the live birds flying again in the sky. This was their link to immortality. In the sun-dances of the Plains Natives and the dances of the Hopi and Navajo, Condor feathers were used to pray to the winged spirit for power and health. Pioneer western miners, Mexican and Native Americans all used their quills that are light and durable to hold gold dust. These feathers held about 10 cubic centimeters of dust in a diameter of half an inch. They closed with a wooden stopper and hung from a thong. Their range once covered most of the United States but by 1987, there were only twenty-seven of these huge birds left in a small area of central California. The remaining ones in the wild were captured and put into captivity in order to try to save the species. There are three units housing these birds; the San Diego Wild Animal Park, the Los Angeles Zoo and the Peregrine Fund's World Center for Birds of Prey in Boise, Idaho. By 1996, there were one hundred and twenty-one birds in captivity as a result of the breeding program.

Condors lay a second or third egg in captivity if the original one is removed so this resulted in the rapid increase of young. Their rate of reproduction is very low and they do not mate until at least six years of age or older. Like all Vultures, they are carrion-eating and do not kill their own prey. The numbers of these birds were greatly reduced by the settling of the West, the building of cities, the loss of their natural environment and the reduction of dead wild animals which are their food supply. Then, too, farmers would leave out poisoned cows to kill wolves and coyotes but alas it attracted the Condors as well. Added to this, many were shot. Their gene pool is now very limited for reproduction and the cost is tremendous to breed them in captivity. Shortly, more of these birds are to be released to join the small number already returned to the wild. They will be placed in the Big Sur and in Southern California where they made their last stand. Two males and four females, all under a year of age were returned to Northern Arizona in December 1996. This makes a second area to be repopulated but the future is still very uncertain for these huge epic birds.

Coot *Fulica 15"*

These circumpolar birds have a membrane between their toes called lobate. This oddity is found in three unrelated species: the Grebe, Phalarope and the Finfoot. Coots like water and nod their heads when they swim. When they fly, they sort of patter along the water into the wind until they get airborne. This pattering may be why they are sometimes called "Blue Peter." To be called "bald as a Coot" comes from the white color above their bills that is very pronounced against their black chicken-like bodies.

To the Pueblo, a stuffed Coot symbolized the stringent taboos under which they placed their clowns. In Horsey, Norfolk, England they held a fair every year called "Coot Custard." All the sweets were made from the eggs of this bird and the Black-headed Gull. In olden times, they were thought to adopt the young of Eagles along with their own and nourished them. They were said to be intelligent and foresighted as they stayed in one place and did not eat corpses. The heart of a "rawe" Coot was a cure for epilepsy. Coots were even placed on the heraldic crests of several families. However, in later years their popularity waned and we got the expression "silly old coot." In eastern Northern Carolina they used to think that these birds turned into Bullfrogs in the summer!

If you insist on eating Coot, you must prepare it well. You strip the feathers and put resin powder on the down and throw it in boiling water to melt the resin. Then leave it overnight in spring water and it will look white and be as delicate as chicken. If you do not follow these directions, the skin will be oily and the bird be dry and uneatable. It hardly seems worthwhile!

Cormorant *Phalacrocorax 15-36"*

This is a large family of thirty species found everywhere but the Islands of the Central Pacific, the northern portions of Canada and Siberia. These dark feathered "Sea-crows" with long hooked bills are found on rocks or pilings with their s-shaped necks and their wings half open. They fly in a sloppy V formation and live near water.

These birds were given a hard time in folklore. The Haida of the Queen Charlotte Islands said that once the Raven asked the Cormorant to go fishing. It seems that this bird caught all the fish and the Raven nothing. The Raven got mad and pulled out the tongue of the Cormorant and that is why he is speechless and songless today. From Europe comes the tale of how this bird was in the wool business and the freighter that was carrying his wool was sunk. That is why the Cormorant is forever diving in hopes of finding his treasure. The Kwakiutl of British Columbia said that one of their ancestors painted all the birds that were in one place. When they came to the Cormorant, all they had left was charcoal, his color today .The Arawak of Venezuela gave this bird a big plus for getting them the pretty colors off a water snake and keeping only the black for himself. The shield of the City of Liverpool, England, depicts a Cormorant with wings closed and elevated; they called it "The Liver." James the First had a Cormorant keeper who trained these birds to catch fish. They were said to have to get their tail feathers wet before they could fly. Another myth said that if one was seen in a church steeple, a shipwreck was happening.

On the more positive side, for centuries the Japanese and Chinese have made good use of these birds. A fisherman would keep about a dozen birds on leather tethers. The birds would be prevented from swallowing fish by a thong tied around the base of the neck. These birds sat on the bow of the boat, and when the throats of the birds were full, they were pulled back into the vessel. There they were stripped of the fish and then tossed back up to the bow again. At the end of the trip, the thong was removed and the bird could fill its throat with fish to eat. However, the birds became so used to disgorging the fish that the fishermen had to retie the thong above the fish or the birds would get nothing to eat. These birds were known as "Shags" from their shaggy plumage at breeding time. They are the "Guarnay" of the West Coast of South America and of great value to man. Their nitrogen-rich guano is mined off the cliffs and shipped around the world as fertilizer.

Cotinga

These birds vary in size from three and a half to eighteen inches and are found in South America. Cotinga is the name that the Amazonian Indians gave to the White Bellbird and means washed white. White birds are usually found in the Arctic regions and not in the tropical rain forests like this bird. The rest of the family of ninety species have unusual colors of purple, red, blue and even some drab ones. The violet shades are from a pigment called cotingin and is not from the usual refracted light of the feather shaft as in most birds.

Cotinga, Pompadour *Xipholena punicea 8"*

This violet-red bird was named for Madame Pompadour because of her elaborate hairdos that often included whole

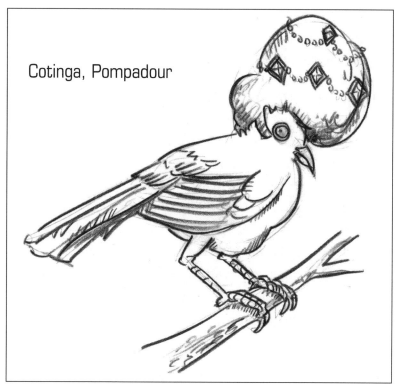

Cotinga, Pompadour

birds and jewelry. The first specimen of this bird to arrive in Europe was sent to her from French Guiana. However, the ship that was carrying the bird was captured by the British. On board was a naturalist-artist called George Edwards who first described it, painted it and gallantly named it in honor of the original recipient.

Cowbird, Brown-headed
Molothrus ater 7 1/2"

The male of this small brown-headed blackbird has a short sparrow-like bill and tilts his tail upwards when walking. His mate is a dull grey. The Hopi used the feathers of this member of the Blackbird family on their prayer-sticks as their arrival meant that it was corn planting time. They did this in spite of the fact that these birds do not make their own nests but lay their eggs in those of other birds.

Crane 38-60"

These long-legged, long-billed and long-necked stately birds are often confused with Herons and Storks. They fly with legs and neck extended and in a V formation unlike Storks. There are seventeen species of these large powerful birds, which are found in warm areas except for South America, the Malayan Archipelago, the Pacific Islands and New Zealand. They need protection as several species are threatened. They can be found in marshlands, wet prairies and plains. The word Crane comes from the Norman "pied de grue" or "Crane's foot." All of these birds have spectacular mating dances where they leap into the air and make many bows and stretches to each other.

From the 13th century onward, they have appeared in the margins of books as decorations and sometimes in scenes of the Creation, the preachings of St. Francis and the Apocalyse. This bird is usually depicted as standing on one leg. The other leg, bent at the knee, has a stone in its foot. The reason was that if the bird fell asleep, the stone would drop and wake it up. Therefore, the Crane became the symbol of vigilance. On their migrations, they were said to carry stones for several reasons. The wind could change direction but the stone in its throat acted as ballast and kept it on course. In the 16th century, people claimed that the stone gagged the Crane so it could not utter cries that would attract Eagles or other Birds of Prey.

The Crane meant a lot of things to a lot of people. In Egypt, they were considered the watchers of the stars. The Greeks said that when they migrated to Africa, it was time to beach their boats and sow the winter crops. When they returned in the spring, it meant sunshine and good weather. It was also thought that when they got to Africa, usually with smaller birds on their backs, they met up with the Pygmies, who rode goats against these birds so that they could steal their eggs. The belief that larger birds carried smaller ones on migrations could be found from Siberia to Africa and Crete to Hudson's Bay.

At Reggio, across from Scilly, there lived many Cranes. When Ibycus the local poet was about to be murdered, he asked the Cranes to witness it. Later, the murderers were in a theater when a flock of Cranes flew over. These men whispered, "The Cranes of Ibycus." They were overheard, arrested and executed. This gave rise to the saying "The Cranes of Ibycus" which was used to express a crime suddenly coming to light. The Greeks and Romans kept Cranes in captivity and sewed up their eyes so as to fatten them for better eating. Their gallbladder was used to cure palsy, consumption and blindness.

These birds have an odd shaped windpipe that gives off resonant sounds that can be heard from far away. The Inuit of Northwest Alaska had the answer as to why they scream and circle around. It seems that one late autumn day, years ago, the Cranes were preparing to go south when they spotted a beautiful girl standing alone. They picked her up and put her on their great wings and carried her aloft. Their brethren circled below so she could not fall to earth. They uttered hoarse cries so the screams of the girl could not be heard. Aelianus had a different answer. He claimed that their screaming was because storms were about to arrive. Their famous ring dance at mating time gave meanings of fertility to several Native American tribes who tried to copy them in their rituals. To some people they were the symbol of death, while others associated them with the sun. Mainly, they were thought of as symbolic of fileal piety.

Crane, Manchurian (Japanese)
Grus japonica

This bird is only really common where the Buddhists protect them. They are a part of their religious and superstitious beliefs. They are easy to tame so are seen in many zoos. In China and Japan, they were a bird of good omen and happiness along with the turtle. Both symbolized a long and happy life. They were used at the celebrations of births and weddings where they placed an image of a Crane on a turtle's back. They are a traditionally long lived bird but the Japanese allotted them one thousand years and gave the turtle a mere ten thousand!

Crane, Sandhill and Whooping Crane
Grus canadensis and Grus americana

The Sandhill is a mainly gray bird of about twenty-four inches while the Whooping is mainly white and stands sixty inches tall. To the Native Americans, these New World birds were just "Cranes." The Pueblo said that these birds protected their clowns and masked dancers so only they could wear their feathers. The Sioux said that they were very vicious and could attack a man but usually picked on a child. They could swoop down and destroy crops leading to suffering and disaster. The Winnebago said that their large bill was very dangerous when they were wounded or at bay. This could be true! Like lots of other birds, when they flew south it meant stormy weather and when they came north again in the spring it meant clearing weather. Very logical. The Crow and the Cree said that they carried a "Crane's-back," most likely a Grebe on their back while migrating. They were said to keep up a constant whistle so warriors copied them when on the warpath. They would blow a whistle to imitate the "Crane's-back" and believed this would preserve them and their ponies from wounds in case of defeat. They would be carried away like the "Napite-shu-utl" or "Crane's-back."

The Whooping Crane was almost extinct in 1941 as there were only sixteen left in the world. With various expensive and controversial captive breeding programs, they have made their way back to approximately three hundred and sixty birds in the wild and captivity by 1996. The best places to see these great birds are on their main wintering ground of Aransas National Wildlife Refuge in Texas and their nesting area in Wood Buffalo National Park in Alberta, Canada.

Crossbill *Loxia 6"*

This bird is in the same family as Grosbeaks, Finches, Sparrows and Buntings, and have seed cracking bills. The male is reddish and the female olive-green with crossed bills. They are irregular visitors in Europe and North America. This bird was known as the "Cruciform bird" as it was said to have gotten its bill twisted and its red color from trying to remove the nails on Christ's cross. Henry Wadsworth Longfellow wrote a poem based on one by Mosem that helped foster this idea.

> "Stained with blood and never tiring
> With its beak it did not cease
> From the cross it would free the Saviour
> Its Creator's son release.
> And the Saviour speaks in mildness

> Blest be thou of all the good!
> Bear as token of this moment
> Marks of blood and holy rood."

In southern Germany, these birds are said to have healing powers and protective virtue. In many places in Europe, they said that its eggs hatched at Christmas and the young flew in full plumage at Easter. They obeyed the master's orders and watched over the mistress in childbirth. They could warn households about fire. In Austria, "cross-birds" were kept in captivity because they could take on human diseases. Birds with the upper mandible bending to the right could transfer colds and rheumatism from a man to itself. If the bill was bent to the left, the same held for women!

Crow 17"
Raven 27"
Corvus

Crows and Ravens are often mistaken for each other in spite of their size differences. In folklore everywhere, they were the symbols of longevity but have always been given a hard time. These two birds and a few others once had white feathers but they were turned black in varying stories dealing mainly with their questionable activities. The Native Americans had differing opinions concerning their habits. They were liked by the Iroquois and some other New England tribes according to Roger Williams of Rhode Island in the sixteen hundreds. They rarely killed one as they were said to be the first birds who brought them grain and vegetables from the sunland. Because of this, they felt these birds deserved a bit of food. They were the sacred bird of the Plains Indians' "Ghost Dance." The Apache had great confidence in them as they signaled the approach of the enemy. However, being black birds, they reminded people of death and a bad Navajo became one on death. They even went as far as to call missionaries "Crows" because of their garments. The Pueblo would not use their feathers on prayer-sticks because of their carrion eating but did use them on masks.

Alexander the Great liked them as they led him across the Libyan desert to the Temple of Jupiter Ammon, where the oracle proclaimed him divine. Two Crows at a Roman wedding were good luck and meant a long and happy life together. If there was only one bird, it was the duty of the attendants to scare it away because the couple saw it as meaning disaster. It was said that on the day that Cicero was murdered, several Crows flew around his head and one got into his bedroom and pulled at the bedclothes.

In hieroglyphics, they symbolized contention, discord and strife. In the days of rebuking women, the church fathers used this bird to tell of the use of cosmetics, false hair, procrastination, vanity and unfaithfulness. In Bohemia, they claimed that this bird pecked out the eyes of St. Lawrence. In northern India, the Crow was supposed to have only one eye that it could move from one socket to another! The French went as far as to say that bad priests were turned into Ravens and bad nuns into Crows. In Europe in midsummer, these birds were said to go down to hell and give their feathers to the devil as a tribute. This idea was based on the fact that the birds were molting and were not so visible. These birds were also weather prophets: "Crow on the fence, rain will go hence, Crow on the ground, rain will come down." Most everywhere they carried the notion of death, thievery or disaster. For example, it would be a bad summer if the fig leaves were shaped like a Crow's foot!

The name Crow turns up often. A "scare-crow" was originally

a sign of the cross to protect gardens. Soon clothes were added and when the rains came they were rendered useless. The words "Jim Crow" obviously came from the black color of these birds. "As the Crow flies" is not always the shortest distance between two points. A "Crow's nest" is a platform high on a mast of a sailing ship, from the fact that these birds nest high in trees. "To eat Crow" means making a very humiliating apology and no one wants to be called "an old Crow." Also, no one wants to get "Crow's feet" meaning those aging lines around the eyes and face!

Cuckoo *Cuculus canorus 13"*

This slim, long-tailed bird of Europe and Asia has two toes forward and two backward. The name comes from the Old English "cuccu", the Anglo-Saxon word "gaec" and the Scottish word "gouk." This symbol of unfaithfulness has been thought of everywhere as a rain bird, rain god or rain crow. A "gouk" storm in the beginning of April meant that the Cuckoo had come back and it was time to plant the oats. The Hindu thought that it was a very wise bird and symbolized the sun behind the clouds.

Frederick Delius's music "On first hearing the Cuckoo's song in Spring" has many meanings attached to it. Some German peasants said that if you roll on the grass on first hearing this song, you will be pain-free for the year. If you have money in your pockets, turn it over and you will have success. If you have none, then you are in trouble. In Wales, a baby born the day the Cuckoo first sings will be lucky all its life. In the Highlands of Scotland and in France, it was unlucky to hear it on an empty stomach! In England, the song would spoil the day of the milk-maid if it was heard before breakfast. In Sweden, they baked cakes shaped like the Cuckoo for good luck. Be sure to stand on soft ground when you hear the song, because if on hard ground you would have problems. As far back as Pliny's time, on hearing the song, you had to draw a line around your right foot and take some dirt from the inside of it. This would keep fleas away wherever you sprinkled it. Also, a young maid on hearing this song, could look for a hair by her left foot in England or right one in Ireland. It would be the color of the hair of her future spouse.

The direction from which you heard this song was very important. In Cornwall, it was lucky if it came from the right. In Germany, it was lucky coming from the south but not the north; from the east signified luck in love and from the west general good luck. On first hearing the Cuckoo's song in the spring in Shropshire, England, the workers would cease their work, put down their tools and head for the nearest pub to drink "Cuckoo-ale."

The most common truth about this Cuckoo is that it lays its eggs in other birds' nests. In Bohemia, the reasoning was that on the day of the Virgin Mary, all birds were supposed to do no work. The Cuckoo disobeyed so was condemned never to know a mother's love or bring up her own children! From Denmark, comes a most interesting answer to this problem. They said that the bird was so busy answering questions from people asking when they would get married, when they would get good luck or how long they would live, that she had no time to make a nest. Aristotle and Pliny had a theory that these birds converted themselves in the fall into the Sparrow Hawk, and then, in the spring, changed back their voices, shape and plumage to become Cuckoos again. This was based on the fact that they vaguely resemble each other but are not seen at the same time of year. The name Cuckoo refers to its song, the cuckoo clock, cuckold (a man whose wife is unfaithful) and to be "cuckoo."

Cuckoo, Black-billed and Yellow billed-Cuckoo
Coccyzus erthropthalmus and Coccyzus americana 12"

These New World Cuckoos are grayish-brown above and white below with different colored bills and long spotted tails. Folklore tells of how when dry weather is ahead, these birds call very unlike their rain-cousins noted above. They are also unlike them in that these birds make their own nests and raise their own young.

Curassow *around 3 feet*

There are seven species of these birds who look like skinny turkeys and are forest dwellers. They were named for the Island of Curacao in the West Indies where they do not exist! The Spanish speaking people of South and Central America, where these birds live, call them "Pavo del Monte" or "Mountain Peacock." These birds are much sought after for their meat which is really delicious and richer and more flavorful than a regular turkey. They are easily tamed but do not breed well in captivity.

Curlew *Numenius 12-23"*

These are long-legged, long-billed shore birds numbering eight species world wide. They are usually told by their long down-curved bills and grayish-brown plumage. The word Numenius stood for the new moon in Greek so it was given to these birds as their bills resembled the new moon! In Europe, they were said to be the "Seven whistlers or Gabriel's hounds" as they contained the souls of the "unchristianed" so were regarded as a death omen.

They are not very good eating as their diet consists of mollusks, small crustaceans and seaweed. In the Middle Ages, you did not carve a Curlew, you "unracked it." In spite of all of this, Henry IV of England in 1399 served this bird when he married his second wife!

In Polynesia, they only used the meat of the breast and thighs, which they marinated in wine and cooked in tomato sauce with sage and bay leaves. This was to cover the fishy taste. The Pawnee were not too fond of them as they claimed that these birds skimmed over the prairies just ahead of the approaching warriors. They twittered to warn the deer and the antelope that the human enemy was coming.

Curlew, Eskimo *Numenius borealis 12"*

In 1910 there was a reference to the fact that, at Cartwright in Labrador, the Hudson Bay Company slaughtered many of these birds. Annually, they put up huge numbers of them in hermetically sealed tins for the company officials in Montreal and London. Two thousand of these birds were found hung up in their store from a one day hunt. This was done year after year. Added to this, these birds migrated along the East Coast en route to South America. There they were slaughtered by more gunners for more markets. It is no wonder that today this bird is probably extinct due to no true sightings.

Dipper

Dipper *Cinclus 7-8"*

There are four species of this truly aquatic bird who likes to go in, out and under the water. They are brown to gray in color with two having some white on them. They can live in this way as their legs are short and strong, have an extra large preen (oil) gland, a third eyelid, and a movable flap over the nostrils to keep out water. They were formerly called "Water-ousel." In 1804, the author of Bewick's "British Birds" invented the name Dipper and it stuck. The author claimed "it perched on top of a stone in the midst of a torrent, in continual dipping motion or short curtsy often repeated." They are not found in Australia or Africa.

Dodo
Raphus cucullatus formerly Didus ineptus
3 1/2-4 feet

This is the most widely known of the extinct birds, probably from its name and the pictures of it by Sir John Tenniel in "Alice in Wonderland." All we have left of this bird who lived on the Island of Mauritius and weighed up to fifty pounds are a few skeletons, two heads and two feet. They had big heads, fat bodies, huge hooked bills, stumps for wings and curly, loose tail feathers. In the 1600s, the East Indian spice traders stopped at Mauritius to replenish their supplies and took vast numbers of these "living flesh pots" as they called these birds. Later, the island became a penal colony and with this came pigs and rats from the ships. These went wild and ate the eggs of the ground-nesting Dodo. The last of these birds died in about 1681, a victim of mankind. Who really was the Dodo?

Dove/Pigeon

The name Dove comes from the German "dubo" meaning a dark colored bird. The word Pigeon is usually applied to the larger species while the Dove refers to the smaller ones. The names are used interchangeably with Dove being the most popular. It was one of the first birds to be domesticated and is found in various customs, art forms, prophetic and sacrificial rituals, as well as being a chief source of food. It was one of the few birds that the Hebrews said could be used in a sacrifice.

At the dawn of civilization, it was a pure bird representing conjugal affection, doing good works and staying married for life. Then it moved on to symbolize the physical indulgence in love and became the bird of Zeus and Aphrodite, the Goddess of Love. It was sacred to Ishtar, a deified goddess of productiveness and coexistent with the male sun god. In nature worship, it combined heaven and earth, male and female. Then came the very dramatic change to meaning the Dove of Christian symbolism - the Holy Ghost. Now it has added to its list the symbol of peace.

As symbolic of the Holy Ghost, it is pictured in church windows as a dove with seven rays of light. These stand for wisdom, piety, understanding, council, fortitude, strength and the fear of the Lord. The Lombards put an effigy of a dove on grave pots because to them the bird was the enshrined soul of the departed. In some Latin countries, on Easter or Whitsunday, doves were liberated in churches to commemorate the descent of the Holy Ghost. In Spain, small cakes were even tied to their legs, before liberating them. This thinking can be seen in the famous Isaac Watt hymn "Come Holy Spirit, heavenly Dove with all thy quickening powers, kindle a flame of sacred love in these cold hearts of ours."

Throughout history there have been many and varied tales of the Dove. Probably the most famous is that of Noah letting one out of the Ark to see if the waters had receded and its return with an olive branch. It also returned with red legs as the heat of the brine singed off the leg feathers so they have been that way ever since. King Solomon was said to have turned two doves into stone because of their boasting, but he still used them as messengers and raced them. Cyrus, the King of the Medes and the Persians, in the fifth century sent messages tied to their feet. Rameses the Third was crowned in 1297 B.C. and sent the news all over Egypt by pigeon. These may have been the first air mail services! Caesar took doves with him on his various wars and liberated them with notes on their legs to tell of his victories. King David got into trouble by trying to catch a beautifully iridescent Dove that resembled precious gems. He fed it and when he thought he could catch it, it flew away. The King's eyes followed it and suddenly he spotted Madam Uriah in her bath. The Dove was famous again when it brought the holy oil for the consecration of Clovis as the first King of France in 496 at Rheims. The news of Napoleon's defeat at Waterloo arrived in England by pigeon four days ahead of the news that went by horse, ship and carriage. When this news reached Calais, Nathan Meyer Rothschild sold his French securities and bought German and English stocks before the news hit the financial markets. This was the start of the House of Rothschild. The famous pigeon of World War I was called "Cher Ami" and saved Whittlesey's Lost Battalion in the Argonne Forest.

There was an old belief in England that a white pigeon was the sign of a departing soul. Gregory of Tours in his "Dialogus" said that the Monks in the Monastery in Nurra saw a dove issue from the mouth of their dying abbot and head for heaven. St. Benedict claimed that he saw the soul of his sister depart as a dove. Thornton Wilder in his book "The Bridge of San Luis Rey" wrote that "the soul can be seen like a dove fluttering away at the moment of death."

Like most birds, doves had medicinal properties. Dovecotes were meant to banish rheumatism. If the birds made more noise than usual, and went in and out more often than usual, there would be a change in the weather. To cure an obstinate fever all one had to do was cut a pigeon in half and apply it to the patient's feet and the fever would leave. There was no indication whether the bird was cooked or raw! If you had pneumonia, you put a dead bird on your chest and you would be cured. People seem to have found therapeutic value in its dung, flesh, blood, feathers or other parts in cases of burns, ulcers, jaundice and most everything else except how to cure being "pigeon-toed!"

Dove, Collared *Streptopelia decato 11"*

They are a very common species in Europe that are sandy colored with black and white on the neck and white bands on the tail. Aelianus said that these birds put sprigs of bay in their nests as a protection against sorcery.

Dove, Mourning *Zenaida macroura 12"*

They are the best known wild pigeon in Central and North America. They are slim, pinkish birds with black spots on the wings and a long tapering tail. The whole family seem to have smallish heads and their wings whirr when taking off. Their mournful coo gave this bird its name. The Pueblo said that they were rain birds who needed water to parch their thirst from eating seeds. Their cooing told of watering places. When they cooed, rain would come down. Their feathers were used in ritual masks used to bring on rain to water the crops.

In Georgia, they were said to be the foreboding of death. If a farmer heard their note above where he was standing, he would prosper, but, if below him, he was in trouble.

Dove, Turtle *Streptopelia turtur 11"*

They are a common European bird and can be told by the white patches and black stripes on the neck. Their name also came from their cooing. In ancient times, they were supposed to live on the crest of mountains as they were shy and shunned man! They were said to live in a hollow tree while they molted. They were so faithful to each other that if one died the spouse would not seek another mate. They obviously could not have been too isolated from people as the food report of 1542 remarked "they make good blood!"

Dovekie *Alle alle 8"*

These Arctic birds are often blown off course in bad storms and turn up inland or further south than usual. These plump little black and white seabirds have a short neck and stubby bill and whirr on rapid wing beats. They are the smallest in the family and are called Little Auks in Europe and "Pineknots" in New England. In Labrador their arrival meant cold weather and they called them "Bonne Homme," or good fellow, but spelt it "Bunnum". In Greenland, they were called "Ice-birds" as they were the harbinger of that season. In Ireland, where they turn up only after a storm, they were considered the originator of the Barnacle Goose legend.

Ducks in general

About one hundred and forty-five species are listed as waterfowl. It is an ancient family consisting of Swans, the largest; the Geese are next in size, followed by the smaller Ducks. The latter seem to break up into these categories: Shellducks, Dipping or Dabbling Ducks, Pochard or Bay Ducks, Perching Ducks, Eiders, Mergansers and Stiff-tailed ones. The word "duck" stands for the female while the male is known as a "drake." In tapestries, these birds are viewed as augurs of the weather. They were sacred to Neptune as they foretold bad winds and often plunged into the water flapping their wings. The Romans had a "nessotrophian" which was a wired, walled, watering place for Ducks that were kept to be eaten or be tamed.

In the seventeen hundreds, bird silhouettes across the moon gave rise to the notion that Ducks and Geese spent the winter paddling the seas of the moon.

The Olmec shaman of ancient Mexico wore a Duck mask, his alter ego, the guise of his human soul. The Cheyenne and Arikerse said that at the height of the Flood, a man was floating around with alot of aquatic birds and he asked them to dive and bring up earth. They all failed except for a small Duck with mud on his beak that he gave to the man. The man then kneaded the mud with his fingers and made piles of it on the water's surface which spread and became a wide plain. The Pueblo hunted Ducks for their feathers and ranked them just below the Eagle and Turkey in importance. The Ducks were said to carry the message of water by joining the earth and the sky.

The Inuit in the Arctic used to amuse themselves in the long winter nights by dividing the gathering into Ptarmigans and Ducks. The former being born in the winter and the latter in the summer. They would have a tug of war and if the summer won then the winter would go away early and hasten spring. If the reverse, then the winter would stay late.

Duck decoys were used as early as the 13th century to lure wild birds to come in to be shot and used for food. The term "duck" has long been used as a term of endearment. "Ducky" was a slang for cute and attractive but degenerated into "just ducky" as pure sarcasm. "Lame Duck" was first applied to a bankrupted stockbroker in the mid-eighteen hundreds in England. In the United States it means a politician who can no longer run for re-election. In other words, "his Goose was cooked." To "duck or ducking" comes from the ducking stools of the 1500-1600s, where they were used as punishment. There was a long pole mounted like a seesaw with a seat at one end to which the offender was strapped, then dipped or dumped into a pool or stream of water. To increase the humiliation of the offender, it could be mounted on wheels and dragged through the streets of the town.

Duck, Black *Anas rubripes 23"*

This bird and the Mallard hybridize freely and you can see the results everywhere. This is the favorite Duck of the sportsman. In 1909 Jack Miner of Kingsville, Ontario, Canada, put leg bands on several of these birds. On these bands were messages from the Bible with his name and address. One of these birds was shot in January 1910 many, many miles away. The hunter was more than surprised to read the words "Have Faith in God." That was a better message than the one put on the first set of bands made for our government in England. Instead of Washington, Biological Survey, they had printed "Wash, Boil, Serve." This resulted in several replies of "No damn good."

Duck, Eider *Somateria 14-18"*

The Icelanders and Norwegians relish these stocky sea ducks for their down and eggs. "Down farmers" have strict laws and these birds are protected. Their down is extremely light and elastic so is great for down covers. The color is mouse grey and not white. The female plucks her down and lays it over and under her clutch until the last egg has been laid. Eggs and down are taken at intervals of a few days so that the bird will continue to lay most of the summer. The farmers know that she has about one and a half nests worth of down. At that point, they let her lay one more clutch of eggs and cover them with the last of her down so that she can raise a family. When she leaves the nest for good, they collect the remaining down. It is fiction that when she runs out of down her mate gives her some of his. He never goes near the nest! The Eider was the bird of St. Cuthburt in Northumbria, England. It was said that these birds got their trust in man by being his companion for the years that he lived alone on the Farne Islands. The Inuits in Labrador used the heads of these ducks to decorate their pouches.

Duck, Gadwall *Anas strepera 20"*

These dabbling Ducks are considered by most people to be the best eating of all Ducks. These mostly grey birds with white bellies spring directly from the water into the air.

Duck, Mallard *Anas platyrhynchos 23-28"*

The variance in size is due to their hybridizing so readily and some have become barnyard Ducks. Their name comes from the French "malart" and were probably the first Duck to be domesticated. A true Mallard is about 23" and can be told by the green head, white neckband and chestnut chest of the male. The Pueblo prized them for their blue-green wing feathers which to them represented the sky and the water.

Duck, Mandarin *Aix galericulata 18"*

In China they are always portrayed in pairs. The brilliant col-ored male and his drab looking female symbolized marital hap-piness. The name "Mandarin" was supposed to have been given this Duck by the British living in China at the time that they were officially named. They are popular worldwide and can be found in ponds of parks where you should look for the gorgeous male. He is really beautiful.

Duck, Muscovy *Cairina moschata 28"*

They are a goose-sized duck with a hissing call that sounds like a small steam engine. Their name came from the Muysca Indians of Nicaragua but somehow got corrupted to Muscovy. A native of Central and South America, they were domesticated by the Andean Indians before the time of Columbus. Now, they have become a barnyard bird and hybridize freely with very odd looking results!

Duck, Pekin *Anas platyrhynchos 23"*

This white Chinese duck is a descendent of the Mallard.

Duck, Pintail
Anas acuta male 28" female 20"

The white-breasted, brown-headed male has a long needle-like tail that accounts for the size variance. Both are slim-necked and the female is dull colored like most "dappling or dipping" Ducks. They feed for food in shallow areas with their tails skyward and head and neck extended downward. They do not submerge. All the Ducks who feed like this have a patch of iridescent metallic feathers in the center of their wings. In Egypt, Pintails were used as a sacrifice to the Sun God Ra and was one of their hieroglyphics.

Duck, Ruddy *Oxyura jamaicensis 15"*

The Aztec said that these birds foretold of storms, because if they beat the water with their wings from evening to morning, the rain would come down. Their tails are long and stiff and usually cocked up to act like a rudder. The male has a blue bill and a pretty white cheek on his large head. They would rather dive than fly and have a hard time walking on land.

Duck, Ruddy Sheld or Brahaminy
Tadorna tadorna 28"

This goose-like duck gave its name to the established church of the Lamas and their abbots wear the colors of this bird. Their clanging call was frequently used in Indian folklore.

Duck, Scoter *Melanitta 19-21"*

Two species of these heavy dark sea birds can be seen along the coasts of the Atlantic and Pacific Oceans while the third one, the Surf Scoter *Melanitta perspicillata* is a North and Central American bird. In 1709, in the South of France, Scoters were eaten. There they were classified as uncertain in origin and so placed with beavers and turtles! The Jews claimed that these birds were "unclean, unhealthy and unsavory." Their flesh is fishy from their food but the Catholic Church allowed them to be eaten in Lent and on fast days as they were closer to fish than fowl!

Duck, Teal *Anas crecca 14"*

This is the smallest European Duck. A subspecies, the Green-winged Teal is a North American bird. They are fast flyers and like ponds and marshes. The male has a chestnut head with a green ear patch outlined in white. In Finnish legends, it was the broken egg shells of this bird that formed the beginning of solid earth!

Duck, Tree *Dendrocygna 21"*

These long-legged goose-like birds are found from the southern United States through South America, eastern Africa and southern Asia. These birds were kept by natives as "watch-birds" as they feed at night and are quick to make alarming noises. They are also called "Whistling Ducks" from their whistle like call. Some of the eight species like trees and others do not!

Duck, Widgeon *Anas americana 19"*

In Portugal these birds are called the "Seven whistlers" from the whirring of their wings and their long clear call notes heard during the night. They supposedly represented the spirits of unbaptised children. This is like the Curlew folktale. Their white crown has given them the name of "Baldpate" in their North, Central and South American range.

Duck, Wood *Aix sponsa 18 1/2"*

They are a medium-sized freshwater Duck. The drake is probably the most brilliantly colored native Central and North American Duck. The female, as in most birds, is dull colored to blend in with her nesting surroundings and harder for enemies to locate. She resembles the female of the Mandarin Duck but the male of both species know which one is theirs. They nest in holes in trees or in nest boxes. When ready to leave, the young just flutter down to the ground and head for the water, unharmed.

Eagles in general

In European literature an "Eagle" could be a Buzzard, a true Eagle or a Vulture. The word "eagle" comes from the French "aigle" and the Latin "aquila". The latter name is derived from their acuteness of sight (acumen) because they were said to see beyond the visions of humans. They became the symbol of the divine, supreme power, majesty, inspiration, thunder, lightning, associated with the sky and various gods, military power, resurrection, baptism, courage, victory and are found on coins and stamps and known as the King of the Birds. To the Norse people, the Eagle was the god of the Wind, a giant sitting in Eagle feathers at the northern part of the heavens. When he spread his wings, the winds would rise from under them. He was the guardian of Valhalla, the banquet hall of the Norse gods. In Egyptian hieroglyphics it resembled the small letter "a" as the top loop looked like an Eagle's head and beak. The swelling circle was his body and his tail was the little line off to the right. He was the Egyptian symbol for king and worshipped as a royal bird by the Thebans in their ceremony at the consecration of a dead ruler. They also thought that he walked with his toes turned in so as to keep his claws sharp. Their gall was mixed with honey as an ointment for the eyes. If an Eagle got sick all it had to do was to eat a tortoise to get well.

The Hindus said that he brought them the sacred drink "soma" from heaven and so Eagle feathers became a talisman for their heroes. In Greece and Rome, the Eagle was the messenger of the gods and thunderbolts were his power. Caesar's uncle Caius Marius gave each legion a gold and silver Eagle to be borne on a pole as a symbol of victory (like the Sumarians, Egyptians and Persians). The Eagle's birthday or day of commissioning was never forgotten. Field sacrifices were held for a victory but often disbanded in defeat. When a Roman emperor died, he was laid on a funeral pyre which was lit and at the proper moment an Eagle would be liberated over the pyre to carry the soul of the deceased to the gods of the other world. The Romans even went as far as to burn Eagle feathers in their fields so that lightning could not damage their crops.

The Two-headed Eagle came to represent the Eastern or Byzantine Empire and the Western or Roman Empire. Charlemagne, the Holy Roman Emperor, in 800 chose the double-headed Eagle for his standard and made the bird face in both directions. Formerly, the Romans had it looking to the right and the Germans had it looking to the left. When the Holy Roman Empire crumbled, the Austrians, Russians and Germans used it until the hammer and sickle came in and in 1933 the swastika. The Eagle was made the symbol of France by Napoleon and he even went as far as to call his little son "L'Aiglon" or Eaglet.

The Eagle is mentioned in the Bible almost as often as the Dove. A good example is from Isaiah 40:31: "they shall mount up with wings as eagles." It became associated with John the Baptist, who on his death was supposed to have gone to heaven on the back of an Eagle.

A popular myth of the Middle Ages tells of how, when the Eagle got old and his wings become heavy and his eyes misty, the bird would search for a fountain. From it he would fly to the heights of the heavens where the sun would singe his wings and evaporate the fog from his eyes. Next, he would dive into a fountain and dip in three times and then would be instantly renewed with the vigors of plumage and vision. This was his connection with John the Baptist and the waters of baptism. The mist myth probably referred to the nictitating membrane of its eyes.

Serpents were said to represent darkness and evil while the

Eagle stood for goodness and light. That is why Eagles were placed on lecterns in churches. The two testaments are represented by their outstretched wings.

In early England, it was thought that Eagle feathers would consume any others placed near them. They were also said to have "aetites" or Eagle stones in their nests. These were said to be made of yellow iron clay and supposedly held magical and sensitive virtues! From the ability of this bird to use it feet, came the ball and claw that we find on the legs of furniture.

One more European myth concerns the King of the Birds. All the birds gathered to decide who would be their king. They finally agreed that the one who could fly the highest would be their choice. All the birds tried but the eagle flew the highest and was about to be declared the winner when off his back flew the Wren so cheating him out of being the King of the birds. In revenge, the Eagle was said to have hit the Wren with his wings and that is why the Wren cannot fly any higher than the hawthorn bush!

The Eagle had many traits that the Native Americans admired, such as speed, grace and power. To them the word "eagle" was loosely used for either the Bald or Golden Eagles. As they were good hunters, many tribes held Eagle dances in hopes of acquiring some of the Eagle's traits. Basically, they made wings of the feathers and attached them to their arms, put on a mask of its beak and a cape of its feathers to cover the head and face. Then they would dance imitating the movements of the Eagle. They also used its feathers and down in headdresses, costumes, prayer-sticks, toothpicks, fans, peace pipes or as talismans of power. To most North American tribes, the Eagle was the keeper of fire, the moon, sun and stars, and when he shook his feathers it caused hail and snow.

The Apache said that all birds were created from the Eagle.

The Eagle was featured in a deluge myth from Minnesota along with the origin of red pipe stone. When the waters rose all the Indians fled to the hilltops but were overwhelmed and perished on the spot. It was their fossil flesh that gave the pipe stone its red color. Only one woman escaped the Flood as her father was the great Eagle. She snatched his foot and got to a lofty mountain, and there she bore twins who were the ancestors of all Native Americans today. The Hopi claimed as their private property the aeries from which they took young birds. The Luiseno of California would use an Eagle or a Condor (if available) in their death dances. The Plains people replaced the Turkey with the Eagle in their fertility rites. They made valuable fans from the wings of these birds. Only a few special warriors were allowed to put Eagle feathers on their shields or make a war bonnet as these feathers stood for comets. The Pueblo said that they were of the sky and could spiral upwards and get lost to the human eye. Being connected with the sky, they were the enemy of the snake below and always the master. The Pueblo also killed a young Eagle at the beginning of the summer so that its spirit could carry prayers for rain to the gods. All the above seems to show that the Eagle is really the King of the Birds in spite of the Wren!

Eagle, Bald *Haliaeetus leucocephalus 31-37"*

This scientific name comes from the Greek "leukos" meaning white and "cephalus" meaning head. Its tail is also white when mature after five years and they have a huge yellow beak. They are common in Alaska, where they sit in trees looking like golf balls. They have just come off the endangered list but are uncommon in the lower United States. Benjamin Franklin wanted the Wild Turkey to be the emblem of the United States but lost out to this bird. The statesman said that Turkeys were good eating, had interesting plumage and best of all were a native bird (so is the Eagle). He said of the Bald Eagle: "a bird of bad moral character; he does not get his living honestly; you may see him perched on some dead tree, where, too lazy to fish for himself, he watches the labor of the fishing hawk (Osprey), and when at length taken a fish and is bearing to its nest, the Bald Eagle pursues him and takes it away from him. Besides, he is a rank coward, the little Kingbird attacks him boldly. He is therefore by no means a proper emblem." However, the Bald Eagle was adopted as the emblem of the Colonies on June 20, 1782, and finally launched at the inauguration of George Washington in 1778. The design has the right claw holding a spray of ripe olives as an emblem of peace and in his left are thirteen arrows to enforce peace, representing the 13 colonies. In his beak is a scroll with the motto "E. Pluribus Unum" — one out of many.

The Pawnee said that it presided in a sacred or holy realm. It guarded rivers from its perch on the cottonwood tree and dove under water to bring up great fish. However, if the Golden Eagle appeared, the "Baldy" abandoned the fish and flew away. The Hopi used the feathers and down of this bird on prayer-sticks. Sometimes they were painted and placed at shrines, springs and altars, reflecting a point of contact with the forces of the supernatural world. The Iroquois said that the Eagle was assigned the tops of mountains because of its strength, acute vision and the fact that the sun could not blind it. This bird was proud, and though he flew to the lowlands to get food, he always flew back to his mountain to eat it. The Pueblo liked his white tail feathers and kept birds in cages to they could be plucked when needed.

Here is the amazing story of "Old Abe," the war Eagle. He was found as an Eaglet by a Chippewa chief in Wisconsin who traded him to a farmer for a bushel of corn. When the Civil War

Bald Eagle

started, the farmer gave him to the newly formed Company C of the 8th Wisconsin Regiment in Eau Claire. They were delighted and called him "Abe." They made him an elaborate perch and a leather thong to keep him there, and hung around his neck a rosette of red, white and blue ribbons. One soldier was made the Eagle-bearer, and in their first skirmish, Abe was in the rear. As the noise did not seem to bother him, he was moved next to the battle flags. He was quiet until the bugle was blown and the guns went off, and then he screamed and spread his wings. At the Battle of Cornish in 1862, the North was suffering many casualties and a bullet severed Abe's thong. He rose up and flew over to the Confederate side and confused their soldiers. Then he headed back to his perch and screamed. This cheered the Northern troops so much that they finally won the battle. He was in front of his troops when they entered Jackson, the capital of Mississippi and was at Vicksburg when it surrendered. One night Abe heard noises in the woods and sounded his alarm, and the troops were able to pick up a Confederate courier; the Union won that battle thanks to Abe. He was in twenty-five battles and even General Grant saluted him when he visited those troops. After the war he was given to the state of Wisconsin and appeared at fairs and benefits for the wounded and their families. At the speeches, he was on the platform with all sorts of Civil War heroes and was very dignified unlike his wartime behavior. He lived until 1881 when a fire broke out in the State House and filled his lungs with smoke. He was known to be 21 years old. They stuffed him and placed him in the State House in Madison.

Eagle, Golden *Aquila chrysaetos 30-40"*

This bird is the national bird of Mexico. The story goes that the Aztec were looking for a place to settle when they came upon a lake with an island in the center. On this island there was an Eagle sitting on a cactus holding a snake. This was a good omen so they settled there and it became the start of their civilization. This bird became their symbol of war. The Eagle and the serpent were very important in their myths. Today, they are both seen on the Mexican flag and on their coat of arms.

It is more of a western bird than the Bald Eagle. It has a seven foot wing span and likes rabbits, rodents, birds and snakes, and can be told by its size and its brown plumage with a golden wash on the head and neck. The Creek used its feathers on their war flags. They made its image in wood or used a stuffed one to be placed on the top of their council lodges. To the Cherokee, only approved warriors could wear their feathers. The Dakota said that only one who had touched a corpse was allowed to wear its feathers. The Iroquois were kinder, saying that it lived in a far away heaven and was chief head of all birds. They claimed that the Golden Eagle never visited the earth but had many assistants upon whom he imposed various duties. The Bald Eagle and the Vulture were two of them. The Natchez and other tribes considered it almost a deity. To the Pawnee, it was known as the monarch of the sky and they called it the Ring-tailed Eagle. Their twelve tail feathers each had distinctive names and are snow white at the base only when immature. These were used in headdresses. The Pueblo and the Sioux also prized those tail feathers of the young birds as they had dark tips which they lose on becoming adults. They took the small feathers from the base of the tail along with the big ones and put them in their ceremonial war bonnets. It was considered bad luck to kill one so they trapped them. This was a dangerous pastime. However, once caught, they were tethered so the owners could get new feathers each year. Our last story comes from the Island of Innis Boffin at the mouth of Killery Bay in Ireland. There they believed that Adam and Eve still roam around there as Eagles.

Eagle, Harpy *Harpia harpyia 38"*

Early explorers were awed by their size and ability to lift monkeys and sloths high into the forest canopy. They called them "harpies" after the predatory monsters of Greek mythology who were half bird and half woman and had a facial disc like an Owl.

In the Pre-Columbian culture, its nesting in the Great Ceiba (silk-cotton) trees, the tree of life for most Mesoamerican cultures, gave it a mystical status and it was called "Winged Wolf." In the cultures of the Aztec, Mayan and Olmec peoples, images of this bird have been found on wall paintings, figurines, jade masks and stone ruins of their civilizations. The Princes of Tlascala wore its image on their breasts and shields as a symbol of royalty. In Mexico, they were trained for the sport of falconry.

This Central and South American bird of eighteen pounds and a wing span of seven feet is now endangered. Its habitat is being threatened by the clearing of forests. While only about 5% of their food are colorful Parrots, the pet traders often kill them as they consider these birds to be in competition with them. This is strictly illegal.

Eagle, Sea *Haliaeetus around 30"*

In the area of the Black Sea, these birds were considered a good omen for the fishermen; so much so, that their image was placed on the local coins.

Egret *Egretta*

These are long-legged, white-plumaged birds of the Heron family who can be found in the temperate and tropical areas. Their scientific name comes from the French word "egrette." Plumes of these birds have been used for centuries for decorations. Only tufts of the feathers from the middle and lower parts of the back were used. They have no stiff barbules so seem soft as silk. These special feathers are called "ospreys" in Europe and "aigrettes" in America. They grow just prior to breeding, a most critical time to collect these birds. Small bunches of these feathers were used as ornaments in front of turbans, on other headdresses and on caftans by persons of high rank. Often they were mounted with precious stones. The gift of an "Egret" by an oriental ruler was supposed to be the greatest of honors. The one sent to Lord Nelson, after the Battle of the Nile, was said to have been more valued by that hero than any other gift that he ever received.

Egret, Cattle *Bubulcus ibis 20"*

These are buffy-backed stocky herons with short yellow bills and dark yellow legs. They appear white except for the brownish patches on the head, back and breast. These natives of Eurasia and North Africa somehow turned up in British Guiana between World War I and II. They did well and started their northward trek through the West Indies and into Florida in the nineteen forties. Today, they are into Canada and have even gotten as far as Australia and Malaysia. They like ruminant animals and forage around their feet for insects that the cattle have dislodged while eating. They also like to perch on their backs—a free ride!

Egret, Snowy *Egretta thula 24"*

This is the bird that is called the "Golden-slippered Egret" because its feet are a bright yellow in contrast to their black legs. They stir up the water with their feet to get their prey and then stab them with their black beaks. These colonial nesting birds assume their lovely "aigrettes" at the breeding season and that was when the plume hunters killed them. In 1848, five hundred thousand Snowy Egrets were killed in Venezuela with their feathers selling for $15 an ounce in the fashion markets. In 1905 and 1908, in Florida, two Audubon wardens were shot by feather hunters. Finally, in 1913, the sale of these feathers was prohibited but not before very few of these birds were left. Luckily, now the population has recovered and you can see these "Golden-slippers" in most marshes and swamp areas of North, Central and South America. It was in Chile that these birds were called "thula," their scientific name today and first described from there in 1782.

Emu *Dromaius novaehollandiae 5-6 feet*

These Australian Ratites have double feathers that are almost equal in size to each other. Though they can weigh 120 pounds, they are fast runners having been clocked at thirty miles an hour, and can swim as well. They can be a pest to farmers as they can knock down fences, trample the crops and eat them as well.

The Arunta of Central Australia had a clan belonging to the Emu totem. In order to increase the supply of these birds, they would clear a plot of flat land, open their arm veins and use this blood to cover three square yards. When it dried and caked into a hard surface, they made the sacred design of the Emu totem, especially of the parts that they liked the best, namely the fat and the eggs. Then they put on a headdress that resembled the Emu's head and long neck, mimicking the bird's appearance by standing around aimlessly peering in all directions. They also hunted these birds for meat which was said to taste like beef and for their fat to be used in oil lamps. Omelets were made from the eggs but first broken into a bowl and left overnight so that the oil would rise to the top. One egg could feed a large family.

Falcon, Peregrine *Falco peregrinus 16-20"*

There are sixteen species of this bird who live in the entire northern hemisphere as well as Australia, South Africa, Patagonia and the Falkland Islands. They are often called "Duck Hawks." Their heads, crowns and napes are black with a black wedge that looks like a helmet over their eyes. This is very distinctive and a good field mark. They have loose-looking thigh feathers and long pointed wings. They hunt from several feet high in the air and swoop down at tremendous speed to clean kill their prey. One of these dives was clocked at 175 miles an hour by a pursuing aircraft.

Henry the IV of France had one of these at Fontainebleau and somehow it escaped and was located in Malta twelve days later some 1350 miles away. Luckily, his name was on one of its legs so it was returned to the monarch. These birds were and still are widely used in falconry. One of these appears in the famous Holbein painting of "The King's Falconer."

Falcon, Prairie *Falco mexicanus 15-19"*

There are 58 species of Falcons ranging from the Pygmy Falconet of the Philippines of six and one half inches to the Gyrfalcon at twenty-four inches. The Prairie Falcon is a western bird and looks like a sandy-colored Peregrine. The shields of the Crow tribe featured this bird because it stood for protection. They painted this bird on their shields and then added real feathers. This bird was the hero of several tales from central California, one of them describing how he rescued his wife and lost his eyes!

Finch

There are many species of these birds and can be told by being small to medium in size and having short, conical, pointed bills that are adapted for eating seeds. They are found all over the world except Antarctica and a few oceanic islands where there are no seed-growing plants. Finches were thought to be cleverer than man about weather changes. People used to blind them to make them sing better. In western Flanders, there was a regular betting game with thousands of people involved. The finches were shut up in glass fronted boxes and the winner was the one who sang only the distinctive ending note of its song. Owners would go to extremes, including the use of drugs, to make them sing only that note. Hence a good bird was worth a lot of money!

Finches, Darwin's 4-8″

These birds were discovered by Charles Darwin on his "Beagle" visit to the Galapagos Islands in 1835. They helped him develop his theories of evolution. There are thirteen species living on the Galapagos Islands and one on the Cocos Island off Costa Rica. These birds are all similar enough to be related but are markedly different. The fourteen species are believed to be descended from a single ancestor. They are a neat clean-cut example of adaptive radiation. The descendants of the original stock radiated and differentiated to fill the ecological niches in the archipelago. The greatest difference is in the shape of their bills. They vary from warbler-like to long and then to stout and finch-like bills. Some are straight and others curved. One species even uses a cactus thorn to pry out insects, then drops the thorn and eats its meal. Another Finch pecks at the developing feathers of Boobies (seabirds) and drinks the blood from the wounds that it makes! The research of Peter and Rosemary Grant on Daphne Major Island has shown that few birds do hybridize. They have watched this happen over a twenty year period! This is very important in evolution and speciation and opens up new fields for research.

Finch, House *Carpodacus mexicanus 5 1/2"*

These birds can be told from the Purple Finch *Carpodacus purpureus* as they are smaller and the males are red and not raspberry in color. Also they are striped on the sides and belly and can show yellow. The females of both are streaked brown.

The Mayans said that when the gods made all the creatures, they had a few pieces left over and fashioned them into Hummingbirds. The only trouble was that they were dull colored, so the male House Finch kindly gave the male Hummingbirds some of his red feathers.

The spread in the range of this southwestern Finch started in 1940 when bird dealers in California shipped these wild birds to New York under the name of "Hollywood Finches." The Fish and Wildlife Service people picked this up as a violation of the Migratory Bird Treaty Act. However, the dealers quickly liberated the birds to avoid prosecution. The birds started on Long Island, found New Jersey and Connecticut and are now all over the northeast and have been introduced into Hawaii. They have thrived in their new locations and in many places have displaced the House Sparrow. This is a plus as they are colorful and have a pleasant song.

Flamingo *Phoenicopterus*

D rawings of these birds have been found on the walls of caves dating from the Stone Age. The name comes from the Portuguese "flamingo," the Spanish "flamenci" and the Latin "flammea" all meaning flame. Pliny called these birds "Phoenicopterus" their generic name today. Their tongues were said to be a delicacy by the Romans and were served at banquets of emperors. Interests do change and next they were sought after for their plumes. Today, they are still eaten by people in marginal food areas but they must be awfully fishy as that is their main diet.

There are four species of Flamingo found in isolated areas of the world, the most famous places being Kenya, the West Indies and some Andean highlands. The largest in size is about four feet tall and all have varying degrees of red in their plumage. They fly with necks stretched out and legs dangling, both of which are long in proportion to their bodies. They prefer brackish or salt water where they build a mud nest 15 feet high and lay one egg. Their bill is unique and they feed with the bottom part on top and the top on the bottom. This is to sieve the water and mud and get a mixture of algae, protozoans, worms, larvae and plants. They are hard to capture as they can swim well and run fast.

Flicker, Northern *Colaptes auratus 13"*

F ormerly there were three Flickers: the Yellow-shafted of the east with the under feathers of the wings being yellow; the Red-shafted from west of the Rockies with its red feathers; and the Gilded of the southwest with its golden under shaft. Unlike most Woodpeckers, these birds can be seen on the ground looking for ants. They dive their bills into ant burrows and then extend their long tongues. It is sticky from a substance from the salivary gland so holds its prey. The red feathers of this Woodpecker were said by many Native American tribes to represent the dawn and the color of the southwest. Some tales tell of how the Raven made these birds out of the blood of his beak that he had bruised. Haida fishermen tied red flicker feathers on their halibut hooks for good luck. The black-tipped salmon-red underwing and tail feathers were sought after by the Pueblo for war symbols. In Taos, flicker and dyed red eagle feathers were placed in the mountains as offering to the Red Bear, the spirit patron of warriors. Red feathers on prayer-sticks were war offerings but if put in the hair had to do with the medicine people. The tail feathers were the most sought after but if unavailable then the wings of **Lewis's, Downy or Hairy Woodpeckers** were used.

Frigatebird _Fregata 40"_

This name comes from their mastery of the seas like the frigate ships of yore. They are one of the most aerial of the seabirds with a seven foot wing span. They are also called "Man-o-war Bird" from sailors watching their swift flight and habit of cruising near other seabirds and pursuing them for their catch. The early Greek and Egyptian fishermen told of how they would swoop down from above and rob their fishing lines of fish. Herman Melville, in his book "Moby Dick," said that they followed ships and swooped down to attack their flying pennants. Many Pacific Islanders considered them to be messengers of the gods, probably because they can soar for long periods of time on motionless wings. In the Gilbert and Marshall Islands in the Pacific, these birds were trained to carry messages from one island to another. They are called "Hurricane-birds" as they are said to fly low when a storm is coming. Another name is "Bos'n bird," a contraction of boatswain as their long tails suggest a marlin spike, a traditional sailor's implement. In the Caribbean, they are called "Siso" as they can open and close their scissor-like tail. In Florida, they acquired the name of "Poison-bird" as they were said to drop a substance that stupefied fish to make them easier to catch!

The male is a large dark bird with narrow wings and a long tail. He boasts of an orange gular pouch which he can inflate. In courtship, it becomes bright red and can be held inflated for several hours. The female has no gular pouch and has white underparts. The young have white heads. Besides heckling other birds for their food, they chase flying fish, jellyfish, squid and others on the water's surface. They have a problem in doing their own fishing as they have no waterproofing in their feathers so could easily drown if they fell into the sea.

Fulmar, Northern *Fulmarus glacialis 19"*

The Inuit said that their race Mother Sedna, a daughter of a chief, was wooed and won by a Fulmar who promised her a lovely home far away. When her father went to visit her a year later, he found that she had been mistreated and misled. He then killed the husband and took the repentant daughter home again. That is why Fulmars still mourn and cry for their murdered fellow.

They are a gull-like "tubenose" whose nostrils extend into their bills in short tubes like the Albatross. These birds fly on stiff wings and are more or less one color of gray. They like following fishing boats for food. The Icelanders called them "Foul mew" which got changed to Fulmar. They were also called "Foul gull"

Fulmar

from their musty smell and habit of spitting out the contents of their stomachs at intruders. The natives of St. Kilda in the Outer Hebrides liked the oil they vomited as a cure for all diseases. They were supposed to feed on whale blubber so could cure both external and internal complaints and they were a delicacy thrown in. In the Faeroe Islands, the Natives were said to draw a wick through a dead Fulmar and light it at one end for a candle as the flame was fed from the fat and oil of the bird. "Birds burning the candle at both ends" probably did not come from this custom but from the high metabolism and short life span of most birds.

Gallinule, Purple *Porphyrula martinica 13"*

These birds were once known as the symbol of chastity. Their name comes from the anglicized version of "gallinula" or little hen. In the days of moats around castles, they had a variety of names such as moor-hen, water-hen, sultanas or purple waterhens. This is because of the color of these chicken-like birds. They are blue, violet, green or blackish in color with red and yellow bills and a blue forehead shield. These colorful swamp birds wade or swim near lakes and ponds and have elongated webless toes to support them on aquatic vegetation. They are found in some parts of Europe and the New World.

Gannet *Sula bassana 40"*

This member of the Booby family was the "ganote" of the eighth century Beowulf and the Anglo-Saxon "ganote." This was the first of its family to be described by the Europeans. The name comes from the same root as gander or male goose. The "sula" is a Scandinavian name for this bird and is now its scientific name. In the 16th and 17th centuries they were considered good eating although small and tasting like herring. In olden times, it was thought that this strongly migratory bird was unable to fly over land. They are goose-like with streamlined bodies, pointed wings, short legs and a straight sharp bill. These black and white birds are like Pelicans in having air sacs under their skin to break the impact with the water when they dive. When John James Audubon visited Bird Rock in the Gulf of the St. Lawrence in 1833, he thought that the rock was covered with snow. In reality it was thousands of Gannets breeding on the rock. In 1869, a lighthouse was built on the rock so it became more accessible to fishermen. They clubbed these birds to death for bait and reduced their numbers to a few thousand. Luckily, the government put a stop to that slaughter and the birds have come back in good numbers.

Godwit *Limosa 16"*

These birds have a long straight or slightly turned up bill. At breeding time their plumage is reddish but becomes whitish in winter. In Europe these birds used to be netted in the spring and then fattened to make them delicious. Even Ben Jonson agreed with the result!

Goldfinch, American *Carduelis tristis 5"*

The Pueblo said the yellow color of this "Wild Canary" was the symbol of pollen so their arrival meant summer was coming. In the mating season, the male is a yellow bird with a black cap, tail and wings with white wing bars. The female is a paler version of her spouse but in winter they look alike. Watch for the color change in spring especially in the male. They are thought of as harbingers of the better weather ahead.

Goldfinch, Eurasian or European *Carduelis carduelis 4 3/4"*

These little red and white faced birds with yellow wings are found all over Europe and Asia and were symbolic of the Crucifixion. Over five hundred paintings were done of this bird in the Middle Ages. The better known are by Crivelli, Tiepolo and Rosselli. They appear with the Mother and Child, St. John, the Nativity, the Adoration of the Shepherds and Magi and

71

occasionally in secular tapestries and paintings. It was said that the red on the bird's face came from trying to pull out the thorns on Christ's crown on the Cross. This idea was probably based on the fact that these birds eat among the thorns and thistles. In European folklore, God painted all the birds and by the time he got to this Goldfinch, he had only fragments left so took all of his paints and used them up on this Finch. They even were said to avert the Plague!

These neat colorful birds have a pretty song and are easily caught and caged. They were introduced into the United States but did not survive though they have done well in Bermuda and New Zealand. In some areas they are still caged and even blindfolded to make them sing better. Children used to tether them by one leg and played with them as toys.

Go-away bird *Corythaixoides concolor 18"*

This gray, brown and white Tauraco comes from South Africa and is related to the Cuckoo family. These birds get the name of "Plantain-eaters" from their diet. This bird's name comes directly from its loud nasal call of "go-away, go-away." It is so loud that it is said to alert game to the presence of hunters!

Geese in general

This name comes from the old English word "gus." To be correct, the male is called the gander, the female the goose and the young are goslings. These birds have played a very important part in mythology and in local folklore of all peoples around the world.

Geese can be identified on Egyptian tombs dating back to 3000 B.C. They were used in decorations, hieroglyphics and mummified as sacred, especially to Isis, the goddess of love. Ramses the First alone offered 360,000 geese in sacrifice over a thirty-one year period. While they were sacred to the God of the Nile, they were still eaten. The Greeks considered them watch-birds and used them as guardians and companions to their children. Penelope, the wife of Odysseus, kept twenty of them. Even Eros, the Greek God of Love, rode on the back of a Goose.

The best known Roman story of the Goose tells of how a flock of them saved Rome in 390 B.C. They were in the temple of Juno where the Roman soldiers were asleep, when suddenly the Gauls under Brennus attacked. The cackling of these sacred birds awakened the soldiers and the barbarians were chased away. Afterwards, the grateful Roman Senate voted that the Geese be maintained on public funds and a golden Goose was carried in a yearly procession in their honor.

Geese have many facets. The Michaelmas Goose was one of the oldest magical-religious ideas, traced back to prehistory and involving ancient fertility rites and even good Saint Martin. One of these birds was the cause of his demise. He fattened up a special Goose, killed it, plucked it, cooked it, ate it and then died. So, on November 11, you should eat Goose to honor the old saint.

The wild Goose was sacred to Brahma in Hindu mythology who was depicted riding on a magnificent gander. The Indian myth of the Goose and the golden egg is often told. The man who became Buddha was born a Brahman, grew up, married and had three daughters. When he died, he was born again as a Goose or Mallard with gold feathers. He gave them up slowly to support his family. One day his wife decided to pluck him clean in spite of the daughters' pleas. She plucked him and his feathers became white and worthless, and when the bird molted again they were white. Then there is the Aesop fable of the Goose that laid a golden egg. The owner, not satisfied with one golden egg, killed the Goose and found only entrails.

Probably the greatest legacy of the Goose was the use of its parts; what they meant and what they could do for people. They were winter weather prophets. In November, if the breastbone was thick, the bad weather was ahead. If it was pink, then there would be a mild winter. A lot of down at the base of the feathers told of bad times ahead. Goose fat was kept in jars for cooking and home remedies. For example, Goose grease and turpentine rubbed on the chest took care of colds, asthma and bronchitis. It was great for baldness as it was quickly absorbed into the skin. The top vertebra of a Goose cured cramps and eased childbirth if it had not touched the ground first! Goose dung mixed with the middle bark of the elder bush and fried in May butter was a salve for burns. If the concoction was kept from May to May, it protected the owners from fire injuries. Its fat was also used as an aphrodisiac. In Egypt, in the Old Kingdom, there are still tomb paintings showing teams of men with huge nets, traps and snares with which to catch these birds. Then they were either eaten or fattened by force-feeding and their organs extracted and made into salves to keep the flies from biting.

In India, a white Goose was the symbol of the sun and soul while in China it stood for light and masculinity. Calling Geese, often heard after they had gone by, gave hints of ghostliness. In rural Maryland, the cackling of Geese meant rain, and if they flew low in Nova Scotia or New Brunswick, it also meant rain. In East Prussia on St. Matthew's Day, the 24th of February, the housewife would not spin as it might harm the Geese. In Sweden and other northern countries, they used the Goose as a grave offering. Goose bones have been found on an ancient Swedish ship. They had either been sacrificed or left there for food for the departed.

On the cheerier side, from Siberia to Egypt and Crete to Hudson's Bay, people felt that these birds carried smaller ones on their backs when they flew north and south. Geese were used in wedding ceremonies in China and patrolled a whiskey factory in Dunbarton, Scotland. You can make a friend out of a dog with a steak but not with a Goose. The saying "what is sauce for the goose is sauce for the gander" means both parties must participate. Who said that a Goose was silly?

Goose, Barnacle *Branta leucopsis 25"*

This name comes from a series of blunders. The Latin "pernacula," the Portuguese "barnace," the French "barnache" and the Scotch "bren-clake" or "Solan goose" were all corrupted into barnacle. Suddenly, this black and white Goose became the

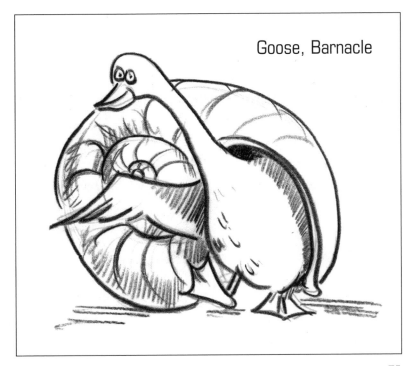

Goose, Barnacle

offspring of small snail. This famous snail is *Lepus anatifera.* Geraldus Cambrensis in 1187 spoke of "broken pieces of old ships in which is found a certain spume or froth, which in time breedeth into shells, and the fish which is hatched therefrom is in the shape and habit like a bird." This mollusk was said to have the general shape and color of a wild Goose with folded wings and hung like seaweed presumably by their beaks from the timber. They were then said to fall into the water or take flight as fully grown birds. Many other so-called learned people said that they had seen the same thing happen. These birds are rarely seen in Europe at breeding time as they nest in the high Arctic and only venture south in the winter.

The Irish bishops of the past said that these birds could be eaten on fast days as they were not born of the flesh. They did not breed, lay eggs or hatch them or even make a nest. Many early authorities agreed but it bothered the Jews because they did not know how to kill them by manner of fish or fowl. St. Jerome went as far as to say that they were cannibals!

Goose, Canada *Branta canadensis 25-45"*

There are many subspecies of this bird so they vary from two and a half pounds to thirteen! They are very common and a pest on golf courses. Many no longer migrate and just settle in permanently. They have plump bodies, short legs and a rounded bill. They are grayish with a black head and neck that carries a white chin strap. The smaller subspecies live the furthest north.

The Cree claimed that Finches were carried on the backs of these Geese to Hudson's Bay. Other peoples said that the Canada Goose carried the Lapland Longspur on its back when it went south and if the Goose was killed, the little passenger just kept on going south. In 1936, there was a newspaper report that a Hummingbird had been found in the feathers of a shot Canada Goose. In the German part of Pennsylvania, they claimed that if you walked on ice on St. Martin's Day, you would walk on mud at Christmas. Also, if it thundered on a Sunday, no Goose eggs would hatch.

Goose, Graylag _Anser anser 35 "_

The Europeans probably domesticated this bird in the late Stone Age or early Bronze Age. It was the ancestor of the domestic Goose of today. In some religions, it was the symbol of fertility and marital fidelity as it mates for life. It is prized for its liver "foie gras" and its warm feathers for quilts. These birds were plucked five times a year and their quills were used for writing pens. They were also very good eating.

"A wild goose chase" comes from their being shy, wary and hard to approach as well as for a useless venture. "You goose" means that you are stupid and comes from the same source as a chicken. They were both domesticated and looked after so needed no brains! "Goose flesh or goose bumps" come on when you are cold and resembles the skin of a plucked Goose. "Goosestep" comes from their stiff-legged waddle. "Mother Goose" probably comes from the mother of Charlemagne and was called Bertha Bigfoot. She may have had big feet but the peasants turned her into a heroine telling stories to her large family to quiet them. The Frenchman, Charles Perrault, towards the end of the 19th century published a children's book called "Tales of My Mother, the Goose."

Goose, Nene or Hawaiian
Branta sandvicensis 23-28"

This gray, black and buff-colored goose is the state bird of Hawaii. They were almost wiped out by the importation of the Mongoose, which are predatory and would eat the eggs of this bird. In 1950, there were only about thirty birds left in the high country of the Big Island, Hawaii. A few birds were sent to Peter Scott's Wildlife Trust in Slimbridge, England, and to a few other preserves. There these birds flourished and several have been returned to their original native habitat where they are holding their own.

Goose, Snow and Blue
Anser caerulescens 28"

This bird has two color phases. One is all white with black primaries of the wings and the other being a dark bodied bird with varying amounts of white on the body. They were once thought to be separate species and now are considered one. Fur traders in Alaska and Canada offered rewards to the natives who saw the first of these Geese returning in the spring. This called for celebrations for two reasons. First, they were a source of new food after a lean winter and, secondly, their arrival was the harbinger of good weather ahead.

Grackle, Great-tailed *Quiscalus mexicanus*

These long keel-tailed blackbirds with yellow eyes live in the southwest United States down to Peru. The males are about 18 inches and the females who are brown are about 15 inches. They are often called "Great Tail or Jackdaw" as their tails are about a foot long.

From the Aztec, we probably find the first species of imported birds to get out of hand. Originally, these birds did not live in Mexico but were introduced in the fourteen hundreds by a Mexican ruler. He insisted that they be fed, no stones thrown at them or any shouting at them. They multiplied and scattered everywhere and soon lost their esteemed position!

Grebe, Pied-billed _Podilymbus podiceps 13"_

This little Grebe lives in the Western Hemisphere as far south as Patagonia. The name comes from the spot on their bills. Their feet are lobate which means their toes are separated by stiff horny flaps with which to propel them in the water. Others who have this structure are Loons, Phalaropes, Coots and the Finfoot. These grebes have a thin neck and appear to be tailless. They can either dive or sink low in the water when needed and have a great habit of carrying their young on their backs.

It was said that Manbush, the mystical ancestor of the Menominee, assembled all the birds by subterfuge and killed several. The Grebe was picked for death as it was a poor runner and easily caught on land. Manbush said "I won't kill you but you will always have red eyes and be the laughingstock of all the remaining birds." Then he gave the poor bird a kick and knocked off most of his tail feathers into Lake Michigan.

Grosbeak, Black-headed
Pheucticus melanocephalus 8"

The word grosbeak comes from the French word "Gros-bec" meaning thick bill. The male of this western species has a black head, cinnamon underparts, white wing patches and a thick bill. The female is buff colored and streaked with the same big bill. In flying both sexes show yellow under the wings. They are one of the few members of this family who have a flight song during courtship and sing on the wing. To the Pueblo bright colors were very important so when these birds arrived back in the spring they brought a nice welcome change to the weather so were much appreciated.

Grouse, Ruffed

Grouse, Ruffed *Bonasa umbellus 18"*

A brown streaked bird that appears chicken-sized can have a red or gray tail. The male has black ruffs on either side of its neck that it can elevate in courtship. The Ojibwa said that the eleven spots on its broad-banded tail are for the eleven days of fasting that disobedient members of their tribe had to suffer. The male makes a drumming noise in courtship displays. He beats his wings without touching his body or the log on which he is standing. A large gathering of these birds together meant snow and if these birds drummed at night then it meant heavy snow. These birds grow "snowshoes" in winter. Each toe gets fringed with a flexible horny point which spreads under its weight to support them on the snow and ice. They are found all over the northern parts of the United States and lower Canada and Alaska and are found in mixed woodlands.

Grouse, Sage
Centrocercus urophasianus 26-30"

This turkey-sized western Grouse has a black belly patch and a pointed tail that he spreads in courtship as well as two yellow air sacs that he also inflates. Like most birds his female is smaller and duller. To most Native Americans, this bird is known as the bird of the morning. The Paiute of the Grand Canyon said that once the whole world was under water except for the summit of Mount Grant on which existed fire. It was the only fire in the world and would have gone out from the wind and rain except for this bird. He settled down and fanned away the water with his wings and so scorched his belly black—it has been that way ever since.

Grouse, Spruce
Dendrogapus canadensis 16"

The male has black on his head and chest with red eye combs that he can erect at mating time. The female comes in a red or gray phase of plumage and they are found in the northern parts of the United States and into Canada. In the Rockies and the Cascade Mountains they are known as "Franklin's Grouse."

The Thompson River Natives of British Columbia would not eat the heart of this "Fool Hen" nor allow their dogs to devour it either. They felt that it would make them foolish like these birds. The reason behind this thinking was the fact that when the young are old enough to fly, they take to the trees when alarmed and make no further attempt to escape. They remain motionless so are easy to kill with a gun or even with a stick.

Guan, Crested
Penelope purpurascens 35"

This chicken-like bird lives in the forests of Central and South America and was given its name by the Carib Indians. The sexes are alike in being olive-brown with a coppery tinge. They have faces and parts of their necks that are bare. When alarmed, they expose themselves to hunters by complaining loudly from a high branch. The natives of British Guinea claimed that after the flood was over, their hero took two sticks and rubbed them together to make a fire. This "Bush Turkey" seeing the sparks thought that the sparks were fireflies so ate one. It burned his throat so ever since his throat wattle has been red.

Guillemots *Cepphus 13"*

These black and white birds of the Arctic are the counterpart to Penguins in the Antarctic. The Hudson Bay and Gaspe Inuits tell of how these birds were created. Once there were a bunch of children playing at the base of a cliff and this bothered the seal hunters. One of them lost his patience and cried out to the gods to make the cliff fall on the children. The God of the Hunters did this but not before the God of the Children turned them into "Sea-pigeons." However, he was not quick enough so some of the children were held captive in the rocks and were turned into Guillemot eggs. This is why these birds lay two eggs unlike the rest of the Auk family who lay but one. These birds nest in rock crannies and keep their young hidden for 6-8 weeks when the young just fly away. These birds were given the gift of molting into white feathers in the winter. This is like the Hare, The Ptarmigan and the Snowy Owl making them well camouflaged from predators. The Aran Islanders used to eat them on Fridays because they never flew over land and lived on seafood. However, they were often slaughtered for fun and left where they were killed, either in the water or on the cliffs.

Guinea Fowl, Helmeted
Numida meleagris 24"

They were named for their country of origin and were domesticated by the ancient Greeks and Romans who got them from Africa. They called them "Numidian birds" hence the scientific name. They are found in the wild south of the Sahara and in Madagascar. The seven species are very similar with bare heads and necks, sleek dark feathers that are sprinkled with white and a short tail. They disappeared in the early Christian era and were unknown until the Portuguese navigators in the 15th century brought them back from the Guinea coast. They are not very productive, and their egg laying is low and they are tricky to raise, but the flesh is excellent. They make a terrible noise so are good watchbirds but their earsplitting voice makes them rather unpopular.

Gull

Gulls are long-winged whitish birds with gray or black wing tips. They are a web-footed water bird that will eat most anything and are good scavengers. They swim well but not under water, are noisy and are great at soaring. There are forty-three species varying from eleven to thirty-two inches. Gull is a Celtic name, and in Scotland and Ireland it was a weather prophet. A common saying was "Sea gull, sea gull sit on the sand, it's never good weather while you're on the land." Sailors said that they were the spirits of dead shipmates and were only lucky when they were sitting on the water. In Elizabethan times, the term "gull" stood for a fool or rogue hence the word "gullible." They were not too popular with some Inuits who claimed that eating Gull's eggs made men old and decrepit!

Gull, Black-headed *Larus ridibundus 14"*

This European Gull is a newcomer to the eastern shores of Canada and the United States. History had it that in 550 A.D. these gulls were flying along the coast of Wales when they came upon a canoe with a day-old baby in it. The child was lying on a pallet and had a folded purple cloth around it. Several Gulls took the cloth and carried the child to a ledge where they nested. Next they plucked their breasts of soft feathers and made a bed and found a doe to give the child milk. Once, when the Gulls were away fishing, a shepherd found the child and took it to his cottage. The doe told the Gulls of this and they came and took it back to the ledge. It grew up to be a man of laughter, singing and happiness.

The young of these birds have been known for ages to be a delicacy. The birds would be driven into nets before they could fly. They were placed in pens where they were fed either liver or corn and curds to give them better flavor. Their eggs were used in cooking and were featured in the old "Coot Custard Fair" in Norfolk, England.

Gull, California *Larus californicus 21"*

These western Gulls were the birds that saved the Mormons in 1848 near the Great Salt Lake. An army of "crickets" had invaded their first crops and started to eat them up. This so-called cricket was the Long-horned Grasshopper *Anabrus simplex Hald* and a favorite of the local Native Americans who ate them. The Mormons were becoming desperate when suddenly a miracle happened. Out of the skies came thousands of these California Gulls who devoured the insects and saved the crops. To thank the Gulls, a statue was erected in Temple Square in Salt Lake City that has two golden California Gulls on the top. The cost was $15,000 which was a lot of money in those days. Naturally, the California Gull is the state bird of Utah.

Gyrfalcon *Falco rusticollis 20-25"*

These very northern ranged Falcons vary in color from almost white in the Arctic regions, especially Greenland, to a browner color as they are found further south with many intermediate phases. They are larger than the Peregrine and frequent open tundra, rocks and cliffs. They are rare everywhere.

In the 12th century in England, taxes could be paid with spurs, animals or with this bird. They were and still are the noblest and best hunters used in falconry. The result of not being common has led to illegal trafficking in these birds and their eggs. The White Falcon is the official mascot of the United States Air Force Academy, which has an extensive set-up for falconry where they train Peregrine and Prairie Falcons and the White Gyrfalcon.

Harrier *Circus 16-22"*

The seventeen species are found in varying places in the world except in the Antarctic, Arctic, and Oceania. In this country it was called Marsh Hawk.

They are long-legged raptors with long square tails and slightly rounded wings and a distinct facial disc. The sexes are unalike. They are birds of the open land, marshes and prairies. The name "Harrier" comes from their "harrying" up and down, back and forth looking for prey. Pliny said of "Circus" that it was "halting of foot, of lucky omen in nuptial affairs and money business!"

Hawks in general

They were said to be the symbol of fierceness, destruction and rapacity. The word Falcon comes from the French "faucon," the Latin "falco" and the Anglo-Saxon "hafec." Probably our first reference to migration and Hawks comes from Job 39:26, "doth the Hawk fly by thy wisdom and stretch her wings towards the South?" The use of Hawks in falconry is very ancient. Trained Falcons were used to fly at prey as early as 2000 B.C. in China. By

1700 B.C. the art had reached Persia. True falconry arrived in Egypt around 800 B.C., in 600 B.C. to Arabia and Syria and finally to Europe in 300 B.C. French falconry in the seventh century had its own scale of values. For example, a bird capable of flying at a crane was worth twice as much as a trained yearling and four times as much as an untrained bird. Marco Polo said of his visit to China that Kubla Kahn's most prized possession was a certain Hawk.

Hawks have always been special birds. In Japan, they told of how a mystical character came ashore from China and as he landed a Falcon came down from the sky and landed on his bow. Ever since they have stood for bravery and success and one is depicted on a medal of victory given to their heroes. Apparently, Hawks for hawking and falconry were first introduced to Japan from Korea in 355 A.D. and given to the ruling monarch. Falconry became so popular that special reserves were created and maintained until about a hundred years ago. The Imperial household kept them on because of their cultural value and interest and had twenty birds at the time of World War I. In the Shogunate days, falconry was ceremonial and traditional costumes were worn. The leg jesses (leather straps to hold the bird) of the Imperial Falcons were colored according to the bird's rank and based on what he had killed. To wear the royal purple, the bird had to kill the large white Japanese Crane several times its size. Other birds wore jesses of red, blue, yellow and brown to signify their prowess and deeds. In Borneo, Hawks were treated as a deity and considered a messenger to a certain God. People asked for their help before working in the fields and before going to war. They even placed wooden images of them in front of their houses to ward off evil spirits.

Falconry was especially popular in England. Soon after the coronation of Elizabeth I and on her birthday, a messenger arrived with a white Falcon adorned with a golden hood as a gift from

Philip I of Spain. By ancient usage, at the coronation of a King of England, the Duke of Athol and Lord Derby presented the monarch with Falcons. There used to be the Office of the Royal Falconer, then known as the Master of the Mews. Anne Boleyn had a white Falcon and Mary, Queen of Scots had a Merlin. Thomas a Becket's Falcon disappeared one day into a swift mill-stream with his talons locked into a Duck. Becket jumped in to rescue it but the strong current took him towards the revolving mill. Some say that the miller stopped the wheel and others said it stopped of its own accord. Everyone agreed that the future saint, martyr, and Archbishop of Canterbury was saved by a miracle! Among other devotees of the sport were Alfred the Great, Edward the Confessor, Harold and William the Conqueror, Edward I and II, Henry the Eighth and James the First.

A hooded Falcon was the symbol of hope. There was a regular hierarchy in falconry. To the Emperor or King belonged the Eagle, the Prince the Gyrfalcon, the Earl the Peregrine, the Lady the Merlin, the Priest and Servant the Sparrow Hawk, the landed gentry and the yeoman got the Goshawk and the peasant was allotted the Kestrel. They claimed that a "falcon" was a female whether "long-winged and noble" or "short-winged and ignoble." The male being about a third smaller was called "tercel." Gyrfalcons and Peregrines were flown against Herons, Ducks, Cranes, Pigeons, Rooks and Magpies. The Goshawk was used for Hares and Partridge and the Merlin for Blackbirds, Larks and Snipe. Often the same name was given to two different species. Much of the sport died with the advent of firearms in the 16th century.

In Punjab, India, their falconers were the most knowledgeable and the bells made at Lahore from a secret process were sought after by falconers everywhere. It was an exacting sport and the twenty-eight species of birds used had to be "broken to the wre" (the lure, an imitation prey attached to a line and "entered" (induced to take prey). The sport is still very popular today. In the 18th century, the village of Valkenswaard in Holland took up the business of getting Hawks and making Hawk furniture. They manned and trained these birds and this monopoly lasted until 1937 when the last of the Mollen family falconers died.

The Native Americans had many Hawk tales as well. The Winnebago had Hawk feathers in every "war bundle." It was a collection of emblems granted by different spirits to the person who had overcome prolonged fasting and had shown power to overcome the enemy in war. The spiral of feathers gave the warrior power to quickly turn himself into a Hawk and his rapid flight would make it possible to easily ascertain the position and strength of his enemy. Some tribes claimed that Hawks had a better spirit than talons as they had so much courage in such a small body. These birds were also said to be Spartan to their young because, when the young were ready to fly, the parents gave them no food and beat them with their wings so that they would learn to care for themselves.

Here is a fun myth of the Yocut of Southern California. Once the world was all water and near Lake Tulane on a pole sat a Hawk and a Crow. They got bored so created birds to prey on the fish. Among them was a Duck who dove to the bottom and brought up some mud, but then he died. So the Hawk and the Crow took the mud and started to make mountains. The Hawk made the East Range and the Crow the West one. After many years of work they were finished and met at Mount Shasta to compare notes. The Hawk found that the Crow's mountains were bigger and that he had been stealing from the Hawk's bill. The Crow just laughed but the Hawk got smart. He took some Indian tobacco and after chewing it became wiser. The Hawk then took

89

the mountains and turned them around in a circle, putting his in the place of the Crow's. That is why the Sierra Nevada are larger than the Coast Range. In one California tribe, they said that small birds who had the bad luck to get the soul of a bad person were chased and killed by Hawks. As a result only good Indians go to the Happy Hunting Ground beyond the sky. So if you were called "hawk-faced" it meant that you were keen and intelligent!

(Hawk) Buzzard *Buteo buteo 20-22"*

This common European Hawk varies in color from almost white to blackish in plumage. In olden times, people distilled the fat from this soaring bird as a cure for sciatica. However, they regarded them with disdain as they were heavy and slow in flight. This gave rise to the term "you buzzard" meaning a stupid person.

Hawk, Common Black
Buteogallus anthracinus 22"

This southwestern U.S. bird has a four foot wing span and chicken-like legs (see scientific name *gallus* referring to chicken). It is often called the "Black Eagle" by the natives as it has a white tail band not unlike that of the Bald Eagle.

Hawk, Cooper's *Accipiter cooperi 14-20"*

The male of this bird and the female Sharp-shinned Hawk are often confused as they both are about the same size, long-tailed and short-winged. Females can be up to one third larger than their mates in several Hawks. The Shavants of the Amazon and the Javante of the mountains of Ecuador made arrows from their primary feathers. This was so the arrows could fly like these birds.

Hawk-Eagle

This bird belonged to one of the principal clans of the Australian aborigines. It was very important to them but is hard to pin down the exact species to which they were referring.

Hawk, European Sparrowhawk
Accipiter nisus 12-15"

In this species the female is bigger than the male. This bird is in a different family from our Sparrow Hawk, now called Kestrel, which is a Falcon and not an Accipiter. This bird belonged to Horus, the Sun God of Egypt and was the symbol of the human soul. It was worshipped throughout that country in the predynastic days. It was said to have been sacred to Apollo. People claimed that it flapped its wings to lure little birds to sleep. The most famous painting of one is that of James the First with one on his wrist.

Goshawk *Accipiter gentilis 20-26"*

This bird of the northern hemispheres has gray underparts and a distinct broad white stripe over the eyes. In Japan, they were the favorite for hunting rabbits and marsh birds. This was because they hit and stay with their prey on the ground and do not strike with their talons. In the feudal days, they were used to kill Cranes. No hunting Goshawk in the Far East could wear the purple jesses until it had killed the Great Japanese or Manchurian Crane, a much bigger bird than the Hawk. John Bricknell in 1737, in his "Natural History of North Carolina," published in Dublin Ireland, said "the dung of the goshawk is exceeding hot, and being drunk fasting on wine, is said to cause conception!"

Hawk, Sharp-shinned
Accipiter striatus 10-14"

This New World Hawk has a slim long tail, rounded wings and appears Jay-sized. Some of the Indian Tribes in Peru paid homage to this bird because of its keen eyesight. The Inca admired it for its courage, swiftness of flight and intelligence. The typical flight of this woodland Hawk is several quick wing beats and then a glide.

Hen, Heath *Tympanuchus cupido 17"*

This was the northeastern seaboard race of the Prairie Chicken. Formerly, they were found in great numbers. In the sixteen forties, these birds were so common that they were constantly fed to the servants. They finally complained about this to Governor Winthrop. By 1791, they were getting scarce and a law was passed to protect them on Long Island but it was disregarded until 1824. By then the handwriting was on the wall - too late. The last bird died on Martha's Vineyard, Massachusetts in 1932.

Herons in general

There are 113 species world wide that vary in size from ten inches to five feet. They are adapted for marsh type living. The name comes from the French "hairon." It was the symbol of Athene while Neptune was said to have deprived these birds of the power to swim! Aristotle claimed that it screamed while "coupling which is difficult and emits blood from its eyes and brings forth painfully and with extreme distress."

It was said to be a good omen and a weather prophet, and it

flew above the clouds to avoid rain. If a storm was coming it would fly away, but if it flew up and down and was unable to decide where to land, then bad weather was ahead. This poor bird was said to wax and wane with the moon. It was plump at full moon but so lean at the change that it could hardly raise itself and you could collect one by hand! To add to these way-out ideas, it was said to keep a crab in its nest as a charm.

These birds have powder-downs, feathers that never shed throughout their lives. They fray at the tip into a powder used for dressing other feathers to remove oil, grease and slime.

In Northern Ireland, if you killed one at the full moon and took its fat, it would cure you of rheumatism. In the Middle Ages, it was claimed to be constant in its diet and not tempted by strange food. Therefore, it was considered to be a faithful believer who paid no attention to alien thoughts!

These birds were used as targets in falconry, were a popular banquet dish and even vows of bravery were made over Herons. A 1542 food report said "a young Heron is lighter of digestion than a Crane." The Native Americans said that they learned the use of the pickax from watching these birds strike at their food—an amazing historical development!

Heron, Black-crowned Night
Nycticorax nycticorax 25"

These short-necked, short-legged Herons are found in the Americas, Europe and Africa. They have black backs and crowns that contrast with their white bellies. These highly migratory birds seem to have their heads set well back on their shoulders. They are often called "Gwowk," "Gwa" or "Gouck birds" from their call.

They were said to be able to throw out light from their white breasts to shine on the water so as to catch fish. Paul Bartsch of the Smithsonian Institution, in 1902, put bands on the legs of twenty-three of these birds. In 1905, he got reports of them from Toronto, Canada and Cuba. These were among the first bird-banding returns.

Heron, Japanese Night
Corsachius goisagi 23"

This Bittern-sized brown bird with pretty black and dark brown streakings sits by day in trees and feeds by night. However, if it gets cloudy or rains, then it will forage for crabs, insects, crustacea and small fish. This is the only bird raised to peerage by the Japanese. According to the legend, the Emperor Daigo so liked its beauty and tameness in his gardens in Kyoto, that he appointed it to the fifth court rank of "Go-i". Today, it is commonly known in Japan as the Goi Heron.

Heron, Tricolored or Louisiana
Egretta tricolor 26"

You can find this pretty bird, who was spared by plume hunters, on the east and gulf coasts of the United States, Central and South America and some Caribbean Islands. Their white bellies and foreheads really contrast to the dark blue upper parts of the body and the chestnut lower back. Its former scientific name *Hydranassa* translates as "Water Queen" but it was sometimes called "Scoggin" in Florida and the Carolinas. This name has been traced to a John Scoggin who was a court fool to King Edward the Sixth from 1537-1553. He was apparently ridiculed as ungainly and uncouth in his actions. What a difference in their nicknames!

Hoatzin *Opisthocomus hoatzin 10"*

This name was derived from the Aztec "Nahuatl." These birds were said to exhale a strong odor, making them known as "Stinkbirds." They are the only birds to have a digestive system like cows. Jungle plants are their diet and they have no problem assimilating them in their huge gizzards. These Amazon Forest residents are brownish with a crest of loosely shafted feathers and eyelashes. Their young have a primitive character in having two well-developed functional claws at the tip of each wing making four limbs for use in the first two or three weeks of their lives. These chicks can swim, and should they fall into the water, they are able to climb out. These extra claws soon disappear leaving no visible sign. In the Amazon Valley, they are called "Cigano" or gypsy but nowhere are they regarded with much favor.

Hobby *Falco subbuteo 11-12"*

This common European Falcon resembles a small-sized Peregrine but with longer wings and a shorter tail. They are extremely graceful flyers, very aerial, and have a dashing type of flight. A relief of this bird can be seen on a grave slab of the Serpent King of the First Dynasty in Egypt dating back to 3000 B.C.

Honeyeaters

These birds are found in Australia, New Zealand and the Southwest Pacific Islands. They number 160 species that range from four and a half to seventeen inches in size though most are on the smallish size. They vary from drab grays, greenish browns and yellow to gaudy black, white and reds. They feed on flower nectar and insects gotten with their slender down-curved pointed bills and long tongues. The feathers of the bright colored birds were used in the feather capes of the Hawaiian chiefs. In some South Pacific Islands, feather money was used and made from the black and scarlet feathers of the *Myzomela* species of Honeyeaters. The 11" Tui of New Zealand has black looking plumage from a distance but in reality it is green, blue and violet iridescence when in the proper light. They display two white patches of curly feathers on either side of their throat. This great singer was therefore called "Parson Bird" but their breast feathers still wound up in Maori cloaks!

Honeyguide *Indicator 4 1/2 - 8"*

These dull colored birds live in equatorial and southern Africa and lead or supposedly lead men to bee's nests. They are said to have a mutual arrangement with the African Honey Badger or Ratel and the natives. The birds get their attention by loud chattering, and when they decide that they have the attention of the follower, they move a short distance. They keep calling loudly with the others following until they come close to a bee's nest. There, the Honeyguide waits quietly for the native person or Badger to get most of the honey and then they move in for the remainder. Their main interest is the honeycomb. They cannot feed their young on the wax as they lay their eggs in other birds' nests, hence do not raise their own young. This interest in wax has to be an inherited trait and not one of parental guidance. There are all sorts of superstitions about this bird so the natives are very careful to leave them some honey. If they did not do so, the birds might lead them to a bad snake or lion!

Hoopoe *Upupa epops 11"*

The name Hoopoe comes from the French "huppe" and the Latin "upupa." These birds live in Europe, Asia and Africa, and can be seen on the walls of ancient tombs and temples in Crete and Egypt. They were one of the "unclean birds" of Leviticus XI:19 because of their eating habits, but in the King James Version the bird was translated as a Lapwing. They seek their food of worms, grubs and insects in dung and do not remove their excrement from the nest. Added to this, they can emit a long lasting smell from the preen gland when their young are threatened. There is a European story of how the Good God offered the Hoopoe millet, wheat and barley for its food. The bird refused them all. At this point the God's patience was undone so he decided to give the bird the worst - droppings!

King Solomon liked this bird as it was supposed to have introduced him to the Queen of Sheba. The King was supposed to have crowned him with a gold crown as a reward, which is what the bird wanted. Soon the Hoopoe found that everyone was trying to steal it so he asked the King to take it back. Instead, he was given a crown of black-tipped cinnamon colored feathers that he could raise and lower.

These so-called nasty birds were said to care for their aging parents who had trouble flying and seeing. They pulled out the old bird's feathers, licked their eyes and took them under their wings until the plumage and sight was restored. Actually, this was the molting process.

They were a sacred bird in Egypt and a symbol of gratitude and still remain so with the Arabs. Their crest was a solar emblem and they were called "Doctor-Bird." The Turks called them "Messenger-birds" from their crest that resembled those

Hoopoe

formerly worn by their couriers. If the Hoopoe sang before the wine harvest, it would be a good season. They were said to stand for marital duty, their heads and hearts had mystical properties in medicine, and they were aphrodisiacs, along with helping in memory and vision.

In England, where it was rarely seen, it was the carrier of evil, but in Sweden it stood for the God of war with its helmet and bright colors. In Italy, it was called "The Little Cock of March" as it was said to bring spring and possess the virtue of divining secrets.

Its habit of eating worms, grubs and insects made it fat in the fall, and it became a delicacy in some parts of Europe and of the Christian population of Constantinople. If you could find a stone in its gizzard and put it on the chest of a sleeping man, it would force him to reveal any sins he might have committed.

Its scientific name is a great expletive - try it - Upupa epops!

Hornbills in general

There are forty-five species of these birds throughout the tropical and subtropical forests of Africa, Southeast Asia and the East Indies to the Solomon Islands and Philippines. They vary in size from two to five feet and are usually black and white with patches of black, white or cream on the tail, wings or body. They have downturned bills that can be horn-colored, black, red or yellow. On the top of the bill, they have casques that are either hollow or filled with combs of cells. These varying sized casques can look chiseled and some are serrated. They all look heavy and some are very gross looking. Some species have bare patches of skin near the eyes and throat. They have strong wings, long tails, short legs and stout feet with three toes partly joined. They have loud carrying voices and some even have eyelashes! Real odd-balls!

All Hornbills, but the two ground-nesting species, nest in tree cavities. When the female is ready to lay her eggs, she is sealed inside the hole nesting cavity with a hole to the outside. This wall is made of mud, dirt and fecal material. They are fairly clean nesters as the female and young void through the hole opening, a new type of one-holer! They are all fed through this hole by the male until the young are ready to take off and then the wall is broken down.

In many places in Africa and Southeast Asia, the people considered their nesting habits with much reverence and would either use these birds or copies of them in their tribal rites of purity or marital fidelity. In some areas they were called "Flying Dogs." In Suba, their meat was eaten as a remedy for asthma and rheumatism. Today, they are no longer hunted and have become sort of a mascot. The casques of the red-nobbed varieties were used in headdresses and on drums when the natives had dances to prepare for war. The red casques were supposed to give the men power and make them invisible! Today, they are used for special ceremonies for dignitaries. In West Borneo, they used to have the Kenyalong dance among the Iban people. Luckily, it only took place every five to seven years as it took eighty Hornbills to supply the needs of the dancers.

Hornbill, Great Pied *Buceros biocornis 60"*

In the forests of Borneo, its profile used to be a symbol of war. These enormous birds have a three foot long tail with a black and white band. The white is frequently stained yellow from the oil of their preen gland but it disappears in death so its not usually seen in museum specimens. These birds boast of lovely eyelashes.

Hornbill, Helmeted *Rhinoplax vigil 50"*

The central tail feathers of this huge bird are about three feet long and were used in belts, caps and ear ornaments by the natives of Southeast Asia and Malaysia. They are dark brown, white bellied with a white tail having a black band. Unlike the other Hornbills, these birds have a solid ivory casque which was used to make ornaments as well as used for fetishes.

Hornbill, Red-knobbed *Aceros cassidix 30"*

This five pound, fig-loving bird is endemic to Sulawesi (Celebes) and adjacent islands. They are fruit eaters and the seeds go through their digestive system unchanged. These are evacuated wherever they fly so they help maintain new growth in several areas. They are especially fond of figs which make up 70% of their diet. The female (like other Hornbills) gets sealed into a hole for the duration of egg laying and the fledging of the young. However, she is sealed in with a mixture of fig seeds and excrement as they live in volcanic areas and no mud is available! The native lore says that you can tell the age of a bird by the number of red chevrons on its bill!

Hornbill, Rhinoceros
Buceros rhinoceros male 48" female 36"

In the Indonesian Archipelago area, the black and white feathers of these birds were much admired. Sixty or seventy of their feathers would be woven into a leopard's skin to make a dancing cloak. They also thought that these birds were the deliverer of souls to the Upper World.

Huia *Heteralocha acutirostris 19"*

This is the Maori name for this now extinct bird of the North Island of New Zealand. The last true record was in 1907 but rumors lasted until 1932. They were a shiny black bird with a broad white band on the tail and orange wattles on the base of a white bill. What made these birds so interesting was the fact that the male and the female had two different bills. Originally, they were thought to be two different birds. The male had a short, stout bill like the Starling so it could attack the more decayed parts of wood and chisel out its prey. The female had a long, very curved bill, like a nectar feeder, so she could go in and probe for grubs. This very specialized feature may have been their undoing, aided by the destruction of forests by axe and fire. In 1870, it was written, "erelong it will exist only in our museums." How very true. There may be only seventy-five specimens found in museums around the world.

The Maori hunters used the white tail feathers for the headdresses of their chiefs, for ceremonies and special occasions. They had special carved boxes in which to keep the feathers as well as the beaks. They used the beaks for head ornament as well as for earrings. Here is a story, told by a Maori in 1900 concerning these birds. A high chief went into the mountains to snare some birds and he came upon a strange one. He plucked out two white tail feathers and put them in his hair. Before liberating the bird, he bestowed upon it a magic spell and manna with the command for it to appear whenever he wanted it. One time when he commanded it to appear, it was nesting time and its tail feathers were in bad repair and all ruffled. When the chief asked the bird the reason for its messy feathers, the bird replied that it was from sitting on its nest. The chief said, "I'll provide you with the means that will enable you to keep your tail feathers in good order for when I call you next." Then he took the Huia, who was a female, and bent her bill into a circular shape. Then he commanded her to lift up her feathers with her beak every time she sat on her eggs so as to keep her tail feathers clear of the nest and remain neat.

Hummingbirds in general

Their name comes from the murmur that they make with their wings when they fly. There are 319 species and they are found only in the New World. They vary in size from the **Cuban Bee** *Calypte helenae* at 2 1/4" and weighing less than 2 grams to the **Giant Hummingbird** *Patagonia gigas* at 8 1/4" and 20 grams from the High Andes. The bills of Hummingbirds vary from straight to curved up or down and are usually dark in color but a few are yellow or red. Their interesting colors are caused by the physical structure of the feathers and not by pigments. Their feathers reflect and absorb light to create those marvelous iridescent colors. It all depends on light, otherwise their feathers appear black. As they are mainly nectar feeders, they are able to adjust their long tongues beyond the end of their bills to collect nectar and insects from the flowers. In order to do this, they are able to fly forward, backward, sideways and up and down and can hover in one spot. There are lots of tales about these birds. Even Captain Cook wrote of their beauty. Most everywhere, people believed that they had special powers, were emissaries to the gods and had strong powers of love. As a result, special potions and amulets were made from their bodies and feathers. Their feathers were woven into cloaks and they were generally known as "Feathered Jewels."

The Arawak of Venezuela said that their ancestors obtained their first tobacco from Trinidad by sending a Hummingbird on the back of a Wood Stork to snatch some seeds. The "Hummer" did just that and put the seeds under the wings of the Wood Stork and flew back home. The Aztec had a powerful God, the Hummingbird Wizard, who was both the Sun and the War God. It was thought that these birds hibernated in the winter by putting their bills in a tree, and that there the birds shrank,

103

shriveled and molted. When the tree was rejuvenated as the sun warmed and the leaves came out, the birds grew new feathers again. When the thunder became rain, the birds would wake up and come back to life! A circlet of their feathers was used as a love charm that was supposed to be effective as well as bringing good luck to the game of chance. The Mayan claimed that their god made all of the creatures and fashioned the Hummingbird out of leftovers. These birds were all gray so the Quetzal, House Finch and the Violet-green Swallow each gave of their brightly colored feathers to these birds.

Today, in Central America, they are still supposed to have supernatural powers and are used as a love charm. Just wear a dead Hummingbird around your neck in a little bag, and you will have great powers to attract the opposite sex. Then you can dry it and put some of the powder in the drink of the person whose love you desire. In Mexico, it was said that, after the Flood, the Vulture was let out and never returned. Then they let out a Hummingbird and it came back with a leaf and all was well. Some natives thought of them as rain birds. Also in Mexico, Montezuma met Cortez arrayed in a long cloak of hummingbird feathers that glistened in the sun. Pictures, ornaments and ear pendants were made out of their feathers and they were also used to decorate temples and idols.

Further north, the Biloxi said that if you asked a question of a Hummingbird, you would get a truthful answer. The Iroquois said that the Moccasin flowers were their shoes. The Navajo had great faith in their swiftness and courage and declared them one of their bravest creatures. There were four animals who brought the original corn to the Navajo. They were the Hummingbird who brought kernels the color of their plumages and that of the Northern Lights; the Bluebird brought the blue corn; the wolf, the white; and the mountain lion gave them the yellow corn.

The Northern Palute had a story of how they sent one of these birds to see what was beyond the sun. He filled his pants with seeds and would eat one each day but he ran out and so returned and said that there was nothing! The Pueblo claimed that these birds resembled rainbows, the arc of which covers the showers coming to earth. As they suck nectar out of flowers and have great endurance and speed, they were said to be messengers to the spirits to send rain. Their feathers belonged to the rain priests who would catch them in snares. The Tlingit claimed that the Raven gave them their beauty. The Winnebago used to say that, by means of fasting and prayer, warriors could acquire the speed of these birds. Once, one of their warriors was wearing Hummingbird earrings and was transformed into one so was able to detect the enemy from a great distance. The Zuni felt that it was a good omen to see one of these birds while running as the bird flew so fast that they would try to copy it. The Hopi made kachina dolls to resemble the Hummingbirds. The final myth is the reason that they really have no voice. It was said that they were so greedy in getting nectar that they lost their voices in the flowers and have been looking for them ever since!

In the 19th century, millions of these bird skins were sent from North, Central, South America and the West Indies to European markets where they were fashioned into ornaments for the ladies. One dealer sent 400,000 skins from the West Indies alone. Bogota, Colombia was the trade center and the birds were known as "Bogota trade skins." From the many species that were sent abroad as commercial skins, eager ornithologists were able to identify many new species!

Hummingbird, Blue-throated
Lampornis clemenciae 5"

The scientific name for this bird comes from the Greek "lampa" plus "ornis" meaning torch bird because of their bright plumage. The male has a brilliant blue throat while the female's is gray. They feed on flower nectar, pollen, beetles, flies plus assorted other bugs and spiders. They love to take spider webs and weave them into their nests. They are native to the Southwest United States and Mexico and are the largest of our North American Hummingbirds.

Hummingbird, Broad-tailed
Selasphorus playcercus 4"

The male of this species makes a sharp trilling noise when he is flying while his partner is silent. The male has a rose-colored throat, green sides and white underparts. The female gets a speckled throat and a cinnamon wash on her flanks and her broad green tail shows red on the outer tail feathers. Both have metallic looking backs. They are found from the Rocky Mountains to Mexico and are affectionately known as "Flowerbirds."

Hummingbird, Ruby-throated
Archilochis colubris 3 3/4"

The male of this eastern Hummingbird has a red throat, green back, grey underbelly and a forked blackish-brown tail. While the female has the same coloring, she lacks the red gorget and has a rounded tail clearly marked with white spots. Foraging

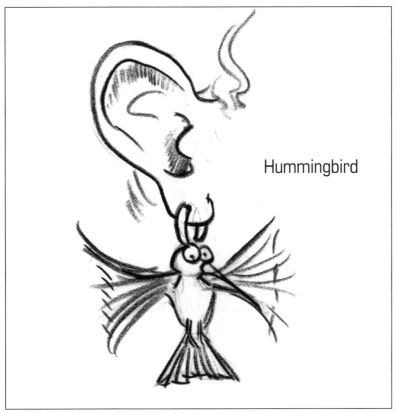

Hummingbird

at a flower can mean they need seventy-eight wing beats per second. They do not need a liftoff as they just take off! The male migrates south well ahead of the female and young. Somehow, they can cross the 500 miles of the Gulf of Mexico on their migrations north and south flying by day.

The Cherokee said that when they ran out of medicine, it was this bird who went far away and brought more back to them. As this Hummingbird is the only one commonly found east of the Rockies, it was their feathers glittering from their ears of the Native Americans that greeted the Pilgrims.

Hummingbird Rufous
Selasphorus rufus 3 1/2"

This early migrant goes as far north as Alaska in February. They have an extensive breeding range in the Northwest of the United States. They are the only Hummingbirds with all rufous backs and green crowns. To this, the male adds an orange-red gorget. They have an unusual courtship display. He has an oval flight pattern. He dives to within inches of the female and then slowly flies upward again. Like the Ruby-throated species, these birds migrate alone some 2000 miles to spend the winter. Their other name is "Sunbird."

Ibis, Sacred *Threskiornis aethiopica 30"*

These black and white birds were sacred in Egypt and played a big part in their religion. The Ibis was venerated as the representative of the God Thoth whose name in hieroglyphics was a figure of a bird. They were supposed to record the lives of every living person. Their white plumages stood for the sun, their black necks were the shadow of the moon, and their bodies and legs made a triangle. They were said to drink only the purest waters and their feathers could scare or even kill a crocodile. Herodotus told of why they were sacred. It seems that, one spring, winged snakes came from Arabia and headed for Egypt. They were met at a gorge by the Ibis who forebade them entrance and killed them. The place was Buto, Arabia. This feat made these birds sacred. Later an investigation of the bones at this gorge showed that they were mammals and not serpents!

These birds were said to destroy scorpions, reptiles, locusts and caterpillars. They also fed on fish but they avoided the strong currents as they cannot swim. These birds would arrive at the rise of the Nile which meant the end of the winds and sandstorms. They stayed in Egypt until the river was overflowing. Today, they are rare in Egypt but can be located in other parts of Africa and Madagascar. To kill one was a capital offense. It was the bird of King Imhotep about six hundred B.C. The king was known all over the Mediterranean as a great healer. When he died, people left mummified Ibis, wrapped in elaborate linens and sealed in a simple red pot. These were left by pilgrims in hopes of absorbing some of the king's healing powers. The sands of time covered the tomb and it was lost. Not too long ago diggers found thousands of these red pots so realized they had located the lost tomb.

These birds were also called "Father John" and "Father of the Sickle" because of the shape of the bill. They did get some mixed reviews however. While it was the symbol of the morning, it was also a mark of a sinner in the Middle Ages. They were said to clean out their bowels with their beak, eat corpses and look for dead fish. They ate so many reptiles that their flesh was said to be poisonous so they were not eaten.

Jacana, Northern *Jacana spinosa 10"*

This bird can be found in Mexico, Central and South America. They are often called "Lily-trotter" and "Lotus-bird" because of their ability to walk on floating plants as they have exceedingly long toes and toenails. They have a bronze-brown body with greenish-olive wings, a red frontal shield and a sharp horny spur at the bend of the wing. The correct pronunciation of this name is "ya-sa-na" with accents on the first and last syllables and a soft "c". This name comes from the Portuguese who got it from the Tupi-Guarani Indians of the Amazon basin who called it "Jassane." The scientific name *spinosa* is from the Latin "spina" for thorn and "osus" for "carrying" meaning the spur at the bend of the wing.

Jackdaw *Corvus monedula 13"*

These birds have gray on the nape and sides of their faces, and a black body. They bob their heads when walking so were said to be a gossip and a thief. Some of this may come from the fact that they love bright colors. If they can find a piece of jewelry, they will weave it into their nest, making a problem for the owner. They are said to stand for vain assumption and empty conceit! Look for them from Europe to Asia.

Jackdaw

Jay *Garrulus glandarius 13"*

The word jay comes from the French "geai" and they were said to be symbolic of senseless chatter. Cicero tells of a Roman barber who had a very intelligent Jay who was capable of imitating musical instruments. Once, during a rich man's funeral, there was a band in the procession with many trumpets and they stayed near the barbershop for quite awhile. From then on the Jay seemed stricken dumb. Neighbors thought that it had been bewitched by a rival barber or that the noise had deafened it. Not so, the bird had been practicing the trumpet notes all by himself and, when he felt that he had mastered it, gave a perfect reproduction of those trumpets in public.

This common, restless European bird that gets as far as Japan, has blue feathers on its wings which were said to be luminescent and shine brightly in the dark. Albertus Magnus said that they could get so mad that they would hang themselves on branched trees. In France, they thought that this bird was subject to falling sickness but still could be eaten if found on the ground! In the Tyrol, they were said to have magic stones in their nests and if you could find one you could become invisible.

In the Middle Ages to "jangle like a Jay" was applied to women who talked too much and its bright plumage stood for a gaudily dressed person. Apparently to "jay-walk" does not come from this bird but from the word "gaius" the Latin for foolish.

New World Jays in general *around 11"*

The Jay was a deity of the Chinook and other Western people. He was thought of as a braggart, schemer, mischief-maker and a real clown. If he was not in trouble for himself, he was making it for

111

others. He had many tricks and pranks and was very comical. The Winnebago called him "Jester" as he went from place to place eating scraps and imitating other birds. People thought if you ate one, your spouse would die. The only people who ate them were very old or unmarriageable. The Tlingit tribe said that he got his crown from the Raven who tied his feathers up on the top of his head.

Jay, Blue *Cyanocitta cristata 12"*

This showy blue and white bird with a crest and white spots on his wings and tail is found mainly east of the Rockies. In the south, he was sometimes called "Satan's Bird" as he never seemed to be seen on Fridays. This was the day that he carried sticks to the devil in hell as he was his messenger. He was very loud and noisy on Saturdays as he was so glad to be back on earth again. The story goes that this was his punishment for his misbehavior at the Crucifixion. No one could tell what he did and anyways he is a North American species! They tell another story of how he got his breast markings. Once, he was yoked to a plow by a sparrow and the so-called necklace on his breast came from that degrading job.

Some people claimed that when the earth was all water, it was the Blue Jay who first found earth. Farmers call him a thief as he pecks at fruits and vegetables. He is good at ganging up on a marauding Hawk. He is said to do this to scare people and have a little fun.

Jay, Gray (Canada)
Perisoreus canadensis 11 1/2"

This gray Jay has a darker crown and a white forehead and is called "Whiskey-Jack" all over its range of Canada and northern United States. This extra name came from "Whiskey-John," originally "Whiskatjan" which was an Algonquin word. The hostile natives of the northern shores of Hudson's Bay claimed that these birds gave warning cries as they approached the Inuit camps. Therefore, they liked to kill them. They have another name which is "Camp Robber" as they are very good at snatching or stealing food. It gets to be a game in picnic areas!

Jay, Pinyon
Gymnorhinus cyanocephalus 10 1/2"

These birds are a steel blue color with a long bill and they act and look like small Crows in their habits and flight. Why not? Jays, Magpies, Ravens and Crows are all in the same family. The feathers of this Western North American bird were used by Native Americans warriors and their priests because they chattered so much. If the warriors wore their feathers, they felt that they made the raiding parties seem much bigger than they actually were. If the natives were unable to locate a crested species, they would substitute the feathers of the **Scrub Jay** *Aphelocoma coerulescens*.

Jay, Steller's *Cyanocitta stelleri 11 1/2"*

This is the only crested Jay found west of the Rockies. It is blue and black and has a long crest. The Pueblo said that this bird represented the west because of its bright plumage and they used its feathers in fetishes. These birds have a great habit of mimicking the Red-tailed Hawk and the Golden Eagle.

Kestrel, American *Falco sparverius 12"*

This is the commonest and smallest North American Falcon and can be seen sitting on telephone wires along roads. They have russet backs and tails and black markings on their white faces. The female's wings are like her back but the male has blue-gray ones. They hover into the wind over the grasses looking for a mouse or grasshopper on which to pounce. The original name of Sparrow Hawk was really a misnomer as they do not usually eat birds. Aspiring warriors of the Pawnee often took their names from this bird. The then Sparrow Hawk was their emblem of war and the messenger to the morning star. They knew this bird as "the Hawk the Gods see." They are easily trained to hunt so they were kept as amusing pets.

Kestrel, Common *Falco tinnunculus 13"*

This common and widespread relative of the New World Kestrel is only a rare visitor to North America. They have bluish heads and napes, reddish backs with spots and banded tails. They were never very popular because they were used by inferior people in the days of falconry!

Kingbird, Eastern *Tyrannus tyrannus 9"*

This New World Flycatcher has a dark back, white breast and a white band at the tip of the tail. The orange feathers in its crown, giving it its name, are rarely seen. This plucky bird is also known as the "Bee Martin" because of its fondness for areas near bee hives. They are famous for heckling Hawks, Eagles and Crows if near their nest. Some Native Americans called them

"Little Chief" from their habits. If you suffered from heart disease, you could be cured by eating the uncooked heart of this bird!

Kingfisher, Belted   *Ceryle alcyon 13"*

This big-headed, big-billed blue Kingfisher lives from Canada to South America and sports a bushy crest. The male has one blue band across its white chest while the female adds an extra rust one. They sit motionless on a perch overlooking the water and then plunge in head first after fish or crustacean, then back to the perch to eat. In Iowa, the Native Americans said that as they brought up food from the water, they should be honored. The Chalam fishermen of Alaska used to tie the skin of a Kingfisher to their halibut hooks for good luck while their neighbors used Flicker feathers for the same reason.

Kingfisher, Common   *Alcedo atthis 7"*

There are eighty-four species of Kingfishers around the world and they vary in size from 5 to 17 inches. This common little bird of the Old World has blue-green upper parts and is orange-red below. They appear to have an oversized head (like most Kingfishers) and a short tail.

There are many tales attached to this bird. It was in Noah's Ark and was let out to see what had happened to the waters as it commonly flew low over the water. However, this time, it decided to go straight up into the sky where its then dull colored plumage underwent a vast change. The blue of the sky was absorbed into its back and the sun scorched its breast red. When the bird returned Noah was mad and kicked it out of the Ark. That is why you will find them in lonely places overlooking the water, like the roof of the Ark.

Another famous tale is that of Alcyone, the daughter of the

115

King of the Wind. She was happily married to Ceyx but he was drowned. Alcyone was so unhappy that her father turned them both into Kingfishers. He decreed that for seven days before and after the winter solstice, there would be calm seas and no wind so they could lay their eggs and raise their young. That was the origin of "Halcyon Days." The Old World Halcyons as they are called, got their name from the Greek "hals" meaning sea and "kyon" meaning conceiving and these were turned into the Latin "Halcyon."

These birds were said to have some amazing qualities as well. People believed that their dried bodies would avert thunderbolts and keep away moths. They were mummified, made into weather vanes, and were known as the "Chief of Fishers." If you hung one from the ceiling by a thread, its bill would always turn in the direction of the wind. William Shakespeare believed this as he wrote in "King Lear": "and turn their halcyon bills with every gale."

Kingfisher, species?

All Kingfishers were sacred to the Melanesians. In Bengal, if you heard one cry on your right side you would have good luck, but if the call came from the left, you would have a failure. This same idea was found in some West African countries and in the south of the United States!

Kingfisher, White-collared
Halcyon chloris 8"

These smallish Kingfishers live from the Red Sea to Samoa and are blue-green above and white below and they are noisy! In China, they used their white body feathers to be set in silver for buckles, hairpins and hat decorations.

Kiskadee *Pitangus 8"*

The Arawak of South America said that this brown and yellow flycatcher got the white spot on its forehead because it put a bandage around its forehead to keep out the noise of the warring animals. The Kiskadee claimed to be sick. However, when the war ended he was exposed as a fraud. His penance was to wear that spot forever. The name Kiskadee comes from the French "qu'est qu'il dit" or "what is he saying?" The romantics say that the call sounds like "kiss me dear." However you translate it, you cannot miss this call from South Texas to Argentina and Bermuda where it was introduced.

Kites in general *Milvus 18-24"*

The word Kite comes from the Anglo-Saxon word "cyta." It was connected with early Egyptian history as their book of religious laws and customs was brought to Thebes by a Kite. The Egyptian scribes wore a red hat with a Kite's feather in it. Kites are medium sized birds of prey with long angular wings, a forked tail and an easy graceful flight. The sexes look alike.

From the Philippines comes another story of the creation. At first there was only the sky and the water. A Kite flew between them and got bored and tired so he decided to make the sky mad at the water. Next the sky made many islands so that the Kite could rest and leave the sky and water in peace. Suddenly, a piece of cane landed on the island where the Kite was resting. The bird split it open with his bill and out came man from one end and woman from the other end. They were married by the consent of the God Bathale Muycapel and from this union came all the nations of the world.

As soon as the Swallows left in the fall, these birds were said to go into hiding all winter. When the Kites came back in the spring, then it was time for the sheep to have their young. There are other tales about this bird. They got sore feet at the time of the solstice and sometimes gout. They detested pomegranates so never went near one of those trees. They were even said to be the symbol of greed and audacity so would snatch food from the hands of children. There is a positive side to these birds. A stick from a nest would cure headaches and if you were a fisherman they were just what you needed. Their tail feathers of light red with a broad band of brown made superb salmon flies!

Kite, Brahminy *Haliaster indus 18"*

This was the sacred bird of the God Vishnu of the Brahmans. They can be found from India to the Solomon Islands and Australia. They have a red-brown back and a white head and are fond of garbage dumps. There they look for small rodents and insects, pick them up with their feet and eat them while flying.

Kittiwake *Larus tridactylus 16"*

The scientific name of this bird comes from the Greek "tridaktulos" meaning three-toed. These are the only gulls found out of sight of land. They range far out at sea after nesting on seaward facing cliffs. They have a square tail and solid black wing tips and call "kittiwake" on the oceans of the Northern Hemisphere. Fishermen used to say that these birds were the souls of young people. As these cliff-nesting birds were easy targets for gunners, they were killed first for sport and then for plumes for ladies' hats. Luckily, laws were passed to protect them so saving these birds from extinction.

Kiwi

Kiwi *Apteryx 16-20"*

This odd looking bird is the national emblem of its native country, New Zealand. You can find their pictures on stamps, currency, textiles, flour and shoe polish. New Zealand soldiers were called "Kiwis" because of this bird's call according to the Maori. There are three species of this flightless, nocturnal bird that looks like a roly-poly chicken. They appear to be all body, feet and legs, with hair-like feathers. Kiwis have the nostril at the tip of the bill unlike any other bird. They have a keen sense of smell which helps them find grubs and worms. For their size they lay enormous eggs that weigh about one quarter of the bird's weight. The Maori chiefs wore long cloaks made from their odd feathers and their skins. While some of these cloaks are over two hundred years old, they still look like new.

Kookaburra, Laughing
Dacelo novaeguineae 17"

This is the largest bird in the Kingfisher family and is found in Australia. There they call it "Laughing Jack-ass" from its loud braying call which has been likened to a madman. It is really a weird noise and they make it mainly at dawn and dusk. No wonder, in the hinterlands, they call it the "Bushman's clock." The natives considered it a deity as it kills fishes and snakes but also has a liking for the young of other birds such as baby ducklings and chicks.

Lapwing *Vanellus vanellus 12"*

The word Lapwing comes from the irregular lag of its wing beat and not because its wings are crossed or lapped. They are a greenish-black and white Plover with a long whispy crest and very rounded wings. In temperate Eurasia, you can see flocks of these birds who seem to start and then stop as they fly.

In Sweden, they were called the handmaiden of the Virgin Mary. The reason being was that this bird was supposed to have stolen her scissors. The bird was punished by being given a tail like a pair of scissors and constantly having to utter a wailing sound of "tyvit" meaning "I stole them." However, in Germany, it was called the "Virgin Mary's Dove." In Scotland, its return in the beginning of March was said to be preceded by several days of bad weather. The 1542 food books said of this bird "it has little nourishment and causes ill humor."

Lapwing eggs, in commerce are known as "Plover's eggs." In 1877, an estimated eight hundred thousand eggs were shipped to England from the Province of Friesland in Holland. These birds are still "egged" in Holland and Belgium but with a cut-off date in May that allows these birds to raise a second brood.

Larks in general *5-9"*

They are essentially an Old World group of seventy-five species. The family name for these birds is *Alaudidae* which comes from the Latin *Alauda* and based on the Celtic "al" for high and "aud" meaning song. They are all brownish with a slightly decurved bill and tufted heads. At one time they were a great delicacy, an example of which is the old Larkspit of the English kitchens.

"We did it for a Lark" means harmless mischief, while "skylarking" comes from the bird's antics in flight and means fooling around. It was originally sailor's slang. Generally, this bird is symbolic of cheerfulness as it is a great songster.

Lark, Horned *Eremophila alpestris 7"*

This is a streaked brownish-gray ground bird with small black horns and a black breast patch. It does not hop but walks aided by its long hind claw, and when it flies it is low and undulating. You can find it in Eurasia, North America, North Africa, Mexico and Colombia.

The Pueblo and Zuni snared, skinned and roasted these birds for food but did not use their feathers. This was unlike most tribes who used the feathers in ceremonies but did not eat the birds. Many Western tribes considered them as oracles. The Dakota's name for them was "Big-ear-tufts." They were said to foretell the weather and bring snow. When a hot day was coming, they would sing only one note but when it was going to rain it had a longer phrase. The Hidatsu said that its name meant wrinkled moccasin because of its habit of crouching on the ground where its cryptic color and black markings made it look like a cast-off moccasin.

Limpkin   *Aramus guarauna 25"*

These large gray-brown marsh birds can be found from the Carolinas to Argentina. They may be the connecting link between Cranes and Rails. Their skeletal structure and feathers are like a Crane but their digestive system and behavior is like a Rail. There is only one species of this bird. The name of this bird is probably Brazilian in origin and comes from its movements. It is said to resemble a limping man even though it is swift and fast. It is also called a "Crying bird" due to its loud strident three syllable wailing note heard mainly in the evening and at night. Limpkins were another bird that was almost wiped out by hunters until laws were passed stopping the slaughter. They were popular as they were easy to catch, being "lame" and very good eating.

Longspur, Lapland
Calcarius lapponicus 5 3/4"

These musical birds of the open country can be found from the circumpolar regions southward to the mid-United States. Their name comes from longspur referring to the spur on its toe which is equally as long and Lapland from the first place that it was described. The Cree said that these birds migrated in the fall on the backs of Canada Geese. If the Goose was shot, the little bird would just continue on its way south.

Loon *Gavia 25-35"*

This name comes from the Icelandic "lomr." All four species are called "Rain Geese" and if they are especially noisy and flying around, then the weather will change. Some people thought that they were heralds or runners of the spirits of the lower regions because they can stay under water for a long time. These sleek black and white birds have pointed bills and are especially geared to swimming and diving. They have solid bones unlike those of most other birds that are hollow. Their legs are attached far back on the body and when they fly their heads seem lower than their bodies. To begin a dive, they just spring up and forward. They can stay under for a minute and sometimes just seem to sink down into the water. In Europe, they are called Divers.

They, too, were mixed up in the Flood and Creation myths. They were said to have brought up soil to make land for people to live on. They were also the messengers of men to the world of spirits and their cry was the spirit of the North Wind. This is why shamans used rattles which were shaped like Loons. The Norwegians said that their call meant that someone was about to drown; and in Northern Europe and Siberia, they were said to escort the souls of the dead to heaven.

The Algonquin thought when they flew around that they were carrying messages to the Master so they would not harm them. The Cree and the Chippewa thought that the call of the Loon meant that they were the messengers of the supernatural. The Ojibwa said that their origins came from the Loon as the voice of their Creator was embodied in that bird.

One of the most popular Native American folktales is that of the blind hunter who appealed to his Loon guardian during a famine. The Loon restored his sight and, in thanks, the hunter gave the bird a gift of his necklace which the bird proudly wears on his breast today.

Many Native Americans made garments of their skin and used the breast and neck patches as tobacco pouches. The Inuit did the same but went even further in using the severed head as a talisman that would endow the wearer with manly qualities. Even the newborn babies had their share of a Loon as they were wiped with the skin of this bird to give them good health and a long life. Their meat is tough and fishy but was eaten when nothing else was around. Their big webbed feet make them sort of shuffle and maybe that is why their name may be a corruption of the old Scandinavian word "loom" meaning a lummox or awkward person.

The word "lunatic" is attributed to this bird. "Crazy as a Loon" comes from its long eerie wailing cry and its antics of swimming under water. There is no question that their call is mysterious and carries great distances and their laughter is crazy sounding. Many people interpret their call as saying "who are you?" It adds up to a mystery with no answer but they are definitely symbols of the wild.

Lyrebird *Menura 38"*

There are two species of Lyrebirds and they are found only in Australia. The Lyrebird is familiar to many as it appears on Australian stamps, coins and on its seal with it tail erect resembling a perfect lyre. They look like a rooster but are brown-backed, ashy-bellied with a long tail, and large strong legs and feet. They are forest birds who scrape the ground for insects and worms while they blend into their surroundings. The male's fantastic tail, when erect, covers his forward body. This is not his usual pose since he only does it for a moment in courtship displays. The male is a great mimic and can copy about twenty birds in succession that might include the Kookaburra, Nightjars and Owls. He can also copy cries of animals and mechanical noises if he so desires. Examples that have been heard include the neighing of a horse, the bleating of a sheep, the whine of a saw and the sounds of cars and their horns!

Magpie *Pica pica 18″*

This black and white, black-billed, long-tailed Jay is the only member of its family to live in both hemispheres. It has long been known as a thief. Generally, this bird has bad thoughts attached to it and it was the symbol of garrulity. It was sacred to Bacchus, the God of wine, so it became associated with intoxication. Its chattering became tattle-telling and as it was addicted to stealing, it became a symbol of ill omen. It all started with Noah who sent it out of the Ark for either stealing or chattering too much. So it sat on the roof of the Ark where it gossiped and this made it an omen of suspicion. The Romans, however, got a big charge out of its stealing and chattering so kept this bird in barber shops to amuse customers. Rossini wrote an opera called the "The Thieving Magpie" whose overture is very popular today.

Various countries have treated this bird differently. In Germany, its chattering meant that guests were coming but they also thought that witches took on their form and rode on their backs. In Northern Europe, the Magpie was said to have the devil's blood in its tongue. However, if you scratched it and added a drop of human blood, the bird would learn to talk. In Perthshire, it was believed that these birds were able to transform themselves into humans. In Yorkshire, you crossed your thumbs to avert its evil; in Sussex, you bowed and removed your hat; and

Magpie

in the West Country, you just plain spat at it! In England, if you saw too many at one time, you could make the sign of the Cross in the air or on your breast, or you could cross your feet and all would be well. Better yet, was to see a Crow and that would break the spell. In the North of England, some people thought that this bird was a hybrid between the Raven and the Dove and was not baptized in the waters of the Deluge so was bad luck. In Brittany, they went as far as to say that Anne, the Duchess of Brittany, their last sovereign, was betrayed by a Magpie. She hid in the carcass of a horse but the Magpie pecked holes in it and so showed where she was hidden. In Wales, if one hovered over the head of a man, he would lose it. (They rarely hover.) If you cut a cross in a tree where they were nesting, the birds would forsake it.

There is a saying about this bird: "one for sorrow, two for mirth, three for a wedding and four for a birth." So you can see that it was not always a "trashed" bird. The Germans said that while it was wholly bad and had motley plumage, it gave warning that a wolf was approaching or else it was the advent of guests. In Scandinavia, at Christmas time, they placed a sheath of wheat tied to the top of the house for this bird. If a fisherman, in the spring, saw only one bird it meant bad luck as it was too cold to leave the nest and eggs. If two were seen then it would be good weather and good fishing.

The English bishops were often called Magpies by irreverent persons because of their black and white vestments. The words "pied and piebald" came from their plumage. The word "pie" came from its messy nest like some baked pies but a "maggie pie" was supposed to be a great treat.

The Pueblo felt that color was very important and that this bird represented the East with its black and white feathers. It suggested dawn to them so they used their feathers on fetishes. They were the emblem of happiness and a favorite bird of the Manchu dynasty. In Oriental folklore, a Magpie nesting near your house was good luck and it was especially good luck to hear one call before you left on a journey.

Lewis and Clark had to contend with their stealing on their way up the Missouri River in 1804. In spite of this problem, Captain Merriwether Lewis, in his diary, praised them for their beauty. He even captured four of these birds and sent them to President Thomas Jefferson as living trophies of that famous expedition. Because of this expedition, William Clark had Clark's Nutcracker *Nucifraga columbiana* named for him and Merriwether Lewis had Lewis's Woodpecker *Melanerpes lewis* to honor him.

Martin, Purple *Progne subis 8"*

All over the world many birds of the Swallow family are called Martins. This bird is found in Canada and the United States and spends the winter in South America. The male is a glossy-purple blue all over while the female and young have white breasts. They are popular birdhouse users but like apartment-style dwellings as they nest in colonies. To the Native Americans, this bird stood for the zenith. They put up hollow gourds on their tent poles to attract them. They did this for good luck and the fact that they are good insect eaters!

Meadowlark, Western
Sturnella neglecta 9"

The Eastern and Western species of this bird appear to look alike. They are chunky brown birds with white outer tail feathers, and yellow breasts that have a black V across them. The best way to tell them apart is to hear their very different songs. Unlike their Blackbird relatives, they are not a flock bird or raider of grain fields or a true lark. They confine themselves to weeds and waste grain seeds. Between them they cover the United States and Canada.

This bird was the most highly esteemed smaller bird of the Western Native Americans. It was regarded as an oracle and they attached words of their own to its song. This singing always told of something. A few examples were where the game was located, news of a wedding or a death, and were always true. Therefore, no one would think of harming this bird or its eggs. The white settlers claimed that its song translated into "you sowed your seed too soon." The Pawnee and the Omaha said that it was endowed with the power of speech. The Pueblo said that its yellow color stood for pollen and was the bringer of summer so they used its feathers in various cures.

The Dakota had about five hundred sayings of this bird and it was one of their favorites. One of their stories tells of a great famine while the tribe was camping near a stream. Suddenly, two spirits appeared and told them where to find the antelope and buffalo. After a successful hunt and much eating, they decided to thank the spirits. They went back to the stream to find them. There they found two Meadowlarks singing sweet songs of faith and cheer. They also believed that in bad weather, if these birds circled up and down, then good weather was ahead. The Dakota of Standing Rock Reservation in the summer of 1918, were said to have interpreted its song as saying that the United States would have a victory. The day before the armistice, they claimed that a late leaving bird said "The President has conquered and the boys are coming home." The Hidatsa thought differently about this bird. They said that the Meadowlark was a scolding woman as she taunted and said aggravating things! In spite of this thought, it is the state bird of Kansas, Montana, Nebraska, North Dakota, Oregon and Wyoming.

Megapode

There are ten of these odd Australian and Malaysian non-migratory ground dwellers. These fowl-like birds have long legs and toes and small short bills. They vary in size from a Hen to a Turkey. They are distinguished by their habit of leaving their eggs in sand or soil, to be heated by the sun or volcanic action, or in mounds of rotting material built just for that purpose. As a result they are also known as "Mound-builders" or "Bush turkeys". Their real name comes from the Greek for "large foot." This is because the male makes a huge heap of vegetation by standing on one foot and scratching with the other. When this is mixed with soil, it begins to rot and generate heat. At the proper moment, at about 95 degrees of heat, the female lays her 6-8 eggs in separate holes and covers them over. She watches and tests the heat each day for eight or nine weeks. Then out pops the young fully feathered and they are then completely on their own. These mounds are often used year after year.

Mockingbird *Mimus polyglottos 10 1/2"*

To "mock" means to ridicule, so when the early settlers landed in the New World and they found this gray and white bird who imitated other birds, they called it "Mockbird." Finally, in 1676, the name was changed to Mockingbird. Its scientific name translates from the Greek as *Mimus* meaning mimic and *polyglottos* as in many tongues. It is the state bird of Arkansas, Florida, Mississippi, Tennessee and Texas.

The Pueblo claimed that this bird gave languages to the tribes, taught them ritual chants and was the interpreter of all that went on in the animal kingdom. The Zuni used their feathers on prayer-sticks and as fetishes. The natives of the Okefenokee Swamp area said that an egg of this bird could stop stuttering. Others said that if a child was slow in talking, the parents should take corn and leave it in the bird's nest for a few days. Then they could take it out, grind it up, moisten it slightly and put it in the child's mouth, and then all would be well.

This bird can imitate about thirty other birds in succession as well as a policeman's whistle or a squeaky wheel. When caged Nightingales from England were brought to the Bok Tower in

Florida and housed in the gardens, the Mockingbirds copied their songs exactly. Thomas Jefferson made a sage observation when he said that the Mockingbird could sing longer than the Nightingale!

Murre *Uria 17"*

The name Murre is derived from the English word "marrot." They are also called "Guillemots and Okpa" by the peoples of the North. Their black and white feathers and red legs make them comical looking but they perform beautiful mating flights and underwater dances so their noisy return in the spring is most welcomed. They lay a single pear-shaped egg on a bare rock. It can rotate but not fall! These circumpolar birds obviously have waterproofed plumage as they live off the creatures of the sea. When a member of this Auk family returns from fishing, it caresses its mate with its bill. Because of this habit, the Inuit claimed they learned to rub noses in greetings from watching these birds!

Myna, Hill *Gracula religiosa 13"*

This bird belongs in the Starling family but are called Grackles in India, which is their native home along with Indo-China and Malaya. These glossy black birds with yellow head wattles have either escaped or have been liberated in many areas such as South Florida. These fruit-eaters are among the best talking birds and are very popular as pets.

Nighthawk *Chordeiles 9 1/2"*

The name Nighthawk comes from the fact that they hunt insects at night. They are slim-winged, gray-brown birds with a white band across their wings. They call in flight unlike the

131

other members of their family. They have an interesting courtship flight where the male dives down from the sky with spread wings at the female on the ground. Next he puts on the brakes and zooms upward again with a loud booming noise made by the wind hitting his primary wing feathers. To many Native Americans, this noise was thought of as a spirit who was calling to them. This is a bit like the courtship antics of the Snipe and Woodcock. They are happy to nest on flat top gravel roofs. Unlike the others in this family, they migrate south in the winter in order to find their needed insect supply. They are found all over the United States. The Pueblo said that this bird was related to the Moon and its pale light and is calling to them. The Huron said that its booming noise made it a Thunderbird. The Nighthawk dance of the Iroquois and Delaware was to give thanks for a healthy growing season. In it they used the wings of this bird. The Zuni used its primary feathers for "strong" prayer-sticks to be used in hunting wars or scalp ceremonies. They also used its feathers as an offering when a newly made field was consecrated.

Nightingale
Luscinia megarhynchos 6 1/2"

This bird gets mixed reviews in folklore. In Europe it was generally thought to be a bird of spring. It was said to be afraid of snakes so it never slept but pressed its breast against a thorn. It sang mournfully so as to keep awake! Ovid declared that Philomela, the daughter of Pandion, the King of the Greeks, mourned so much for her children that she was turned into a Nightingale. The Philomela legend has been in literature three thousand years and is usually connected with grief and forlorness.

There is a Christmas story of a little brown songless bird near the stable when Christ was born. When this Nightingale heard the angel choir, it awakened and suddenly discovered its own voice. Ever since then it has been singing out of the darkness. St. Francis of Assisi was said to have spent a whole night alternating his song version with that of this bird and finally conceded that he had lost. The Italian peasants said that in the beginning God painted all the birds. This bird was the last one and as all the bright colors had been used up, it was given the gift of song. From Finland, France, Germany and parts of England comes the story of how the Nightingale and the Blindworm each had but one eye. The Nightingale stole the Blindworm's eye to go to a wedding and never returned it. As a result, the Blindworm vowed to catch the sinner asleep and recover his eye. That is why the Nightingale has to sing all the time so as to keep awake. This very unimpressive looking member of the Thrush family who lives in Europe gives a lot of song for a small bird and can do it day and night. In spite of all its so-called sins, Jenny Lind was delighted to be called "The Swedish Nightingale."

In tapestries, these birds were said to be symbolic of good weddings. However, it could be a sign of either a happy or unhappy love and could tell of love-making that was not always legal. Now if you want to improve your voice, all you have to do is to eat Nightingale tongues!

Nightjar-Goatsucker family *7-11"*

The colors of these birds are muted browns and grays that blend in very nicely with the ground. They have large eyes, and tiny bills that have large rectal bristles with which to catch and hold insects. Their legs and feet are small and of little use so they fly everywhere even when moving a few feet! In this country, many people would not harm any member of this family because they believed that they were receptacles for departed human souls who have come back to earth. They were said to be here either to haunt their cruel and hard-hearted masters or were unable to rest because of the crimes done in their former lives.

Nightjar *Caprimulgus europaeus 11"*

The word Caprimulgus when translated means goatsucker. Aristotle claimed that these birds flew to the udders of she-goats, sucked at them and made them wither and the goats go blind; hence, the name. Actually, they are just catching the insects stirred up in the grass by the feeding animals. The name Nightjar came from their voice that was so loud that it "jars the night." Their peculiar cry and nocturnal habits of feeding and calling have given them a bad name. In Yorkshire, they called these birds "Corpse-hounds" as they were thought to be the souls of unbaptized infants condemned to wander through the night!

Noddy *Anous 13-16"*

These very pelagic Terns are found in the tropical Atlantic, Pacific and Indian Oceans and breed on isolated islands. They are a sooty brown-black with a white cap and a wedged tail. They got their name from the sailors as they seemed to have no fear of man so were considered stupid. The word "nodden" was used by Chaucer and was the old form of nod such as dropping one's head as in falling asleep. This resulted in the word "noodle" being ascribed to the head. These birds deserved a better name!

Nutcracker, Clark's
Nucifraga columbiana 12"

These Western United States Jays are built like a small Crow with a light gray body and large white patches on black wings and tail. They prefer the evergreen forests and often live above the timber line. They eat all sorts of things, from insects, grubs, nuts, seeds, eggs and young of other birds to picnic scraps. They can easily open pine cones by holding them with one foot and hacking at them with their strong bills. They love to store nuts and cones for future use and if forgotten help reforest mountain regions. They can be quite tame. This is one of the two birds that were named for the famous Lewis and Clark Expedition of 1805.

Nuthatch, White-breasted
Sitta carolinensis 5 1/2"

The word Nuthatch comes from their habit of getting nuts and putting them in the crevices of the bark of trees. There they hammer them with their bills to get them open. Their scientific name comes from the Greek word "sitta" which originally referred to both Woodpeckers and Nuthatches. Finally, in Roman times, the name was assigned only to the Nuthatch.

These birds are found from Canada to Mexico and are usually seen in pairs. Their faces and breasts are all white, and their backs are gray with the male's cap being black and the female's gray. Otherwise they look very much alike. They are very fond of suet and sunflower seeds at feeders. As they go up and down trees head first, they are often called "Upside-down birds."

The Pueblo thought differently about these friendly little birds. They felt that anything that went upside down or backwards

135

was a war trait and that was not normal! Some people even called them "Devil Downheads" as they were dare-devils to go down a tree head first.

Oilbird *Steatornis caripensis 13"*

They are the "Guacharo" from the Spanish meaning "one that wails and cries and grates on human ears." The natives of Northern South America and Trinidad claimed that these raucous semi-human groans that came from the caves where these birds live, meant that the souls of the departed were confined within. These birds cling to the sides of the caves like Swifts and come out at night. These cinnamon-brown birds with white spots have a sonar device in their ears like bats to measure direction by reflected sound waves. They are the only member of the Goatsucker family who are fruit-eaters, preferring the oily fruits of the palm trees.

In spite of the native's beliefs, the young birds were sought after with torches and long poles with which they collected them and then slaughtered them. The young were taken while still in the nest and when they were just big masses of fat. The natives extracted the grease from the birds by melting them in pots over fires near the entrances to the caves. Next, they ran the grease through earthen pots and preserved the result for cooking and for lamps. The end result was said to be pure, free from smell and taste, and it would keep for a year. Maybe this is because they do not eat insects! In Trinidad, the young are considered a delicacy but not so the adults.

Oriole, Northern (Baltimore)
Iectrus galbula 8 3/4"

The word Oriole comes from the French "oriol" and the Latin "aureolus" meaning golden color plus the Greek for jaundice "ikteros." If you had that disease you went to look for this bird to be cured. There are Old World Orioles from the *Oriolidae* family and the New World Orioles who are related to the Blackbirds. This North American bird got its name from the family of the English nobleman, Calvert, Lord Baltimore. He founded the City of Baltimore in 1632 and 1633 and his colors were orange and black, just like this bird. Naturally, it was named the state bird of Maryland. Formerly, the more western species Bullock's Oriole and the Baltimore Oriole were considered separate species but are now lumped together as the Northern Oriole. The Pueblo said that the color of these birds was that of pollen and so when they arrived back in the spring, everyone was happy.

Osprey *Pandion haliaetus 20-24"*

These birds range all over the world except for the polar regions, southern South America and New Zealand. Their backs are black, their breasts and heads white, and they have broad pointed wings. Their thighs are heavily feathered and their legs bare. Their toes are of equal length instead of unequal. Their outer toe is reversible as in Owls, so the birds can grasp with two toes going forward and two backwards. This "Fish Hawk" soars over the water until it sees a prey and then plummets down feet first, wings half closed and splashes. He then shakes off the water and flies off with the fish (hopefully) headed forward and in his talons. Their name comes from the Latin

137

"ossifrage" or bone-breaker but this bird eats only fish! Albertus Magnus claimed that this bird swam with one foot which was webbed and captured its prey with the other that had talons! This was believed for generations until Carl Linnaeus around 1760s shot a couple and examined them. This bird was said to have the power of alluring fish to the surface of the water by means of an oily substance from its body which fish could not resist. Added to this was the thought that it could see distinctly at night so was able to pursue its prey. In Italy, it was known as the "Leaden Eagle" because of its sudden descent into the water after its prey. They likened it to falling lead. The Pueblo called it "Water Eagle" and were correct in their feelings that it was a better fisherman than the Bald Eagle. The Rolti Island Natives, north of Australia, said that the flood was caused by the rising of the sea. They claimed that the Osprey sprinkled earth on the water, made land and brought seeds and fruits to replenish the earth again. Some people thought that if you saw an Osprey circling high in the sky and suddenly it plummeted down that there would be a change in the weather and a thunderstorm.

Conservation programs and the banning of DDT have stopped their decline along with platforms erected for their nesting use. They have made a good come-back in the last few years. Believe it or not, this bird is said to return to the Eastern Shore of Maryland on St. Patrick's Day!

Ostrich *Struthio camelus*

These are the largest birds in the world, eight feet tall and weighing about 300 pounds, and are now only found in Southern Africa, zoos and Ostrich farms. The word Ostrich comes from the old English "estridge" and the French

Ostrich

"autruche." There are many stories about these birds. Albertus Magnus said "it is not much of a bird, but a link between flying animals and small flying birds." He also said that the bat was the link between animals and small flying birds.

The "Physiologus" tells of how the Ostrich looked into the sky to see when the Pleiades were visible in June and it was hot. Then the bird dug a hole in the ground, deposited its eggs, covered them with sand and left so the heat of the sun could incubate them. This is probably based on Job 39:13-14, "gavest thou the goodly wings unto the peacock? or wings and feathers to the ostrich? which leaveth her eggs in the earth and warmth them in dust."

Another story was that they laid their eggs in the sand and the female just gazed at them. If she suspended her gaze for even a moment, the eggs would addle and be thrown out. This idea led to the hanging of these eggs and olive oil lamps in mosques to signify God's watchful eye over man and that he would be dealt with if he erred.

The idea that they hide their heads in the sand comes from the young freezing still in their camouflage plumage and the adults stretching out their necks in the sand to rest on the ground or dig for water. In an emergency, these birds run away on fast legs and kick backward so they are not stupid. Their so-called ability to eat iron probably came from the coins thrown at them in gladiator fights in Rome. The truth is that if they swallow too much, they will die. In Heraldry, they were depicted as holding a passion-nail in their beaks (emblem of the church militant), or horseshoes (a reminder of knightly prowess on horseback) or keys (signifying religious and temporal powers). The Arabs went so far as to say that these birds never drank water.

These birds were useful too. Aside from fighting gladiators, a roast Ostrich was a fitting main course for an emperor's feast. Their eggs were carved and painted and used as drinking cups or bowls and canteens for desert dwellers. The shell is about a quarter of an inch thick and one egg is equal to fifteen or twenty hen's eggs. One of them would make an omelet for eight people and the shell holds about forty ounces of liquid. The feathers from their annual molt are used as ornaments, the skin for fine leather gloves, purses and shoes and the meat for good eating. The Ostrich plume in Egypt was the sacred symbol of justice. The Masai and Zulu used their plumes in their outstanding upswept headdresses and the Knights of the Crusades used them to decorate their helmets. Ostrich feathers have been used as a royal badge since the 14th century. The heraldic crown of three plumes worn by the Prince of Wales dates back to the days of the Black Prince. Even the Pope used some in his fan on Easter. Medically speaking, swallowed stones were used for eye problems and Ostrich fat and sinews were useful tonics.

Ostriches are easily domesticated and do well in captivity and on farms where they can live to be fifty years old. They can be trained to pull carts and to ride but are of no use as draft animals. They tire easily and just sit down and quit. They can be bad tempered, untrustworthy and ungainly pets. They were supposed to be the symbol of stupidity. "Hospice," which was in the 12th century a monastic guest house for "the welfare of man in this life and salvation in the next," came from an inn in Colnbrook in Hants, England. This name came from the word Ostrich.

Owls in general *5 1/2 - 26"*

There are 137 species of Owls in the world. They have forward facing eyes set in a facial disc, with a sharp beak, in a big head on a short neck! Their plumage is soft and fluffy and their flight is noiseless. Like the Osprey their outer toe is reversible.

The word Owl comes from the Anglo-Saxon "ule" and the German "eule". This bird has always been a problem for people, mainly because they come out at night, you do not hear them fly, they have binocular vision, they hoot and hiss and can make semi-humanlike noises and lastly haunt desolate places.

They have played a definite part in the folklore of all peoples. The Greeks liked them but not so the Romans. Nycteme was a Roman girl who lied to her father so was turned into an Owl. Juno picked the Owl as her bird as it reigned at night and was equal to the eagle, who by day was the bird of Jove. The deaths of

Augustus, Aurelius and Julius Caesar were all foretold by the hooting of an Owl. Pliny said, "Bubo (Owl) is a fatal bird, of evil omen beyond all sorts, especially at public auguries; it lies in desert places, and not merely those that are unpeopled, but those of hard access: monster of the night it never utters a song but only a groan. It never flies where it intends, but is borne off at a slant." Pliny the Younger said however, "I know myself that it has perched upon many houses of private men and yet no evil followed."

The Jews did not like them as they said their cries caused death to children. To nullify this, they would pour water into the courtyard every time they heard one so as to distract the cries from the attention of the children. In Egypt, its hieroglyphic symbol meant death. Generally, its eyes were said to be evil as it is almost blinded by day but can see at night. This meant that it never could find the truth! St. Jerome said that it was a "false deity" and it was one of the unclean birds noted in Leviticus.

Agotholes, the Tyrant of Syracuse, in the third century B.C. used Owls to win against a more powerful Carthaginian force. He liberated many Owls among his men and they landed on their helmets. This gave the soldiers inspiration as the bird was sacred to them so they won the battle. In Chinese lore, they were evil birds as the young devoured their parents. Owl soup was served to vassals by feudal lords and emperors to strengthen their loyalty. The soup was supposed to act as a purge of all disobedience. They also put Owl figures on roof tops to keep away lightning. In India, its flesh was regarded as an aphrodisiac but it could likewise turn a man into a fool. In Australia, killing an Owl meant a woman's death and killing a bat was the same for a man.

Throughout Europe, there are varying tales showing how unpopular the Owl was. Probably, the best known one is that of the baker's daughter who stole some of her mother's bread that she was baking for Jesus. Because of this sin, she was turned into an Owl. In Scotland, it was bad luck to see one during the day in spite the fact that some Owls hunt by day. From the Hebrides, comes the idea that if an Owl screamed over your house, it would mean death unless you called out "pepper and salt for your mammy!" In Ireland, if one got into your house, it was killed so that it could not carry away any good luck or tell of any family secrets! In Wales, its hooting presaged death and told of the loss of virginity of some local maiden and the hooting told the time thereof. The Spanish said that once it was one of the sweetest singers but it was present when Christ died and has shunned the daylight ever since and has only the sharp note of "cruz."

The Owls tops the list of birds in its medical properties. In Persia under the Mongols, you boiled the flesh and fat in borax, saffron and vinegar. Then you dried it and beat it and it would then remove any sores from your body. To go to sleep, you put both of its eyes in water and you ate the one that sank and it would work. Not so the other one. If your face was paralyzed, you rubbed its warm blood into your skin. Its warm heart helped too. To kill lice, you applied the warm blood mixed with oil. If colic was your problem, then you ground up the crop, pounded it and then ate it. To stop bed-wetting, you took the bile of the Owl and the ashes of the burned tamarack tree and consumed some at bedtime. To solve migraine problems, you mixed its marrow with the oil of violets and dropped it into your nose. Wasps would fly away if you put Owl dung on the fire. If you had a memory problem, you just hung an Owl over your head and you would be cured. To get sober, you should eat an Owls' egg and if you broke Owl's eggs into the cup of a drunkard, he would suddenly hate drinking! An old medical prescription said "thus the feet of bubo (Owl) burnt hard plumago" and was held to be a help against serpents. If the heart of an Owl was carried by a warrior, he would be strengthened in battle. Some people claimed that if you ate Owl eyeballs, you could see in the dark. You put Owl feathers on yourself if you wanted a deep sleep and drank its broth to cure whooping cough. Soup made from its bones when the moon was waning would cure epilepsy. Finally, salted owl cured gout and Pliny believed an "owlet" was the remedy for leech and insect bites.

The hooting of the Owl was a bad omen so to stop it turn your pockets inside out or any other clothing, or tie a knot in your handkerchief or throw salt on the fire. If the bird was moving its head from side to side, it was weaving a silver thread of moon beams. If you fixed your eyes on an Owl and walked around and around it, the Owl would follow you with its eyes until its head twisted off its body!

To the natives nothing happened naturally but was caused by evil spirits or witchcraft. To the Aztec in Mexico, from 1200 to Montezuma's death in 1521 and their conquests by Hernando Cortez, religion and warfare were their lives. During human sacrifices, stone containers with an Owl motif were used by the priests to hold the hearts torn from the prisoners and offered to the Gods. Drums, with an Owl face carved from a hollow log, would beat the tempo of these gory ceremonies. Their God of the Underworld was symbolized by the night Owl. The Mayan said the Owl was the symbol of stillbirth. Though owls were not generally popular, the Mochina Indians of the coastal river villages in Peru 300-888 A.D. appreciated them. They displayed Owls catching mice on their ceramics as a helper in saving their crops from the rodents. Today, the Inuit make stone cut prints, sealskin stencils, copper engravings and carvings with the owl as a common motif. The Algonquin considered the Owl as a symbol of wisdom and an attendant of the Lord of the Dead - "wise as an Owl." The Apache were very superstitious and placed the remains of their dead in caves that were usually inhabited by Owls whose screech was terrific and heart-rending. They believed that the souls of the departed were reincarnated into small Owls who could listen to the voices of the dead.

The Hopewell of Ohio, 500 B.C. to 500 A.D., made tobacco pipes from pipestone. These and flint stones have been found in mounds and the carvings on them were of the Great Horned, Screech and Long-eared Owls. The Kiowa said that their medicine men on death were turned into Owls and then into crickets! The Pawnee used them in their medicine dances. They wore an Owl fully preserved on their breasts with the beak pointed upward and the tip of the wings extended backwards over their shoulders. To the Pima of the Southwest, the Owl was the symbol of the souls of the dead. If an Owl hooted, it meant early death to a person. So he or she was given a feather from an Owl to help in the journey to the next world. The medicine men kept a supply but a fresh one was the best! A bad Navajo could in death become an Owl or a Crow. The Wichita called the Owl the "Worst Witcher" and were afraid of it but still used their feathers. The Winnebago used Owl down in sacred ceremonies but dyed it red for the Gods. They knew the Owl not for his wisdom but as an old man. The Zuni of New Mexico made earthen water jugs and effigies of Owls and often kept them as pets. Finally, a new wrinkle. Both the Tlingit and their neighbors the Haida, said that the Owl spoke their language because an ancestress of theirs was turned into an Owl for being selfish. Each to his own on the subject of Owls.

> "A wise old Owl sat in an Oak;
> The more he saw, the less he spoke;

The less he spoke, the more he heard,
Why ar'n't we like that wise old bird."

Owl, Barn *Tyto alba 15-20"*

It is often called "White Owl," "Church Owl" or "Monkey-faced Owl" because of its color, nocturnal habits and its heart-shaped facial disc. This worldwide bird has a pale face with dark eyes, long legs, light colored plumage and is rarely seen by day. It has an interesting habit of lowering its head and moving it from side to side. This may be because it hunts more by sound than by sight. In Morocco, where the Jews and the Arabs are not too friendly, they both agreed that it was the bird of Satan. In a Pennsylvania German book of 1819 it said, "If you lay the heart and the right foot of a Barn owl on one who is asleep, he will answer whatever you ask of him and he will tell you what he has done!"

Owl, Barred *Strix varia 20"*

The Penobscot said that his bird was the guardian of their camps. The Florida Seminole would whistle at it when it hooted. If they got no answer, then it meant bad luck but if it called back then it meant good luck. In many places, counter magic was used to neutralize its evil. Examples were to tie a knot in your handkerchief, apron string, turn a pocket inside out or even put your clothes or apron on backwards. All of these helped. If this night Owl called by day, it was a sign of fire so you had to put salt, pepper and vinegar on the fire and it would give the Owl a sore throat and it would hoot no more! These dark barred-breasted birds, with streaking down the belly, were often kept by people. They clipped their wings so that they could not fly but instead do a good job of keeping down the number of insects, slugs and mice around the place.

Owl, Burrowing *Athene cunicularia 9"*

These little Owls can be found in Florida, the West Indies, the Western United States as far south as Tierra del Fuego. They are long-legged, live in open areas, golf courses and prairies, and nest in burrows that they dig. They are usually found in small colonies and if disturbed bob and bow. Often one is standing like a sentinel by the burrow. The Pueblo Zuni called them "Priests of the Prairie Dogs" because the two can live together in peace. They also found this Owl to be droll as it is active both day and night.

Owl, Collard Scops *Otus bakkamoena 9"*

This almost totally nocturnal Owl is found in the Palearctic and Oriental regions. The Ainu of Japan called it "Dear Little Divinity." They associated it with darkness, seers and alchemists.

Owl, Eagle *Bubo 27"*

This large ear-tufted bird with yellow eyes was worshipped by the Ainu. They considered it as a divine ancestor and called it "Servant of the World." They drank toasts to it before a hunt so that they would be successful. They used its head and skin in some of their special ceremonies. The Romans claimed that if the heart of this bird was applied to the left breast of a sleeping woman, she would reveal her secrets. Once, when this common bird got into the Roman Forum, the whole city went into mourning over its foreboding and the place had to be purified in a special ceremony

147

to avert doom. Another Roman said that this Owl, unlike other birds, came out of the shell with its back first as the other side was heavier due to being weighed down by the great size of its head!

Owl, Great Horned *Bubo virginianus 25"*

The Central American, Mayan and Mexican people used them in motifs in their pre-Columbian designs. The Creek held a "Horned Owl" dance in September. The Pueblo thought that this bird was like a tiger, either good or bad. The Zuni said placing one of its feathers alongside a sleepless baby by day would make it sleep like an Owl. Several New World naturalists of the past, like Charlevoix, said that the Owls of Canada laid up a store of mice for the winter. They did this by breaking their legs so that they could not run away. They fattened them up and had them when they needed them. This myth was finally denied and proven false by Alexander Wilson. This common large Owl has big ear tufts that look like horns!

Owl, Little *Athene noctua 9"*

This Old World Owl has an undulating flight and is quite common. This little bird was said to be very wise and was the bird of Athene. It was also the symbol of Athens and was placed on their coins from the first century B.C. to the 6th century A.D. It was said to milk ewes like the Goatsucker but was smart enough to place a bat's heart in its nest to keep away ants!

Owl, Long-eared *Asio otus 15"*

This Owl is found in the Old and New Worlds. They are slender with close together ear tufts and down-streaked breast

Little Owl

feathers. They look at a distance a bit like a Crow. An omelet made from its eggs was supposed to be a cure for drunkenness. Near Bordeaux, France, the country people put salt on their fires when they heard it cry so as to counteract any evil effects that it might carry. They were even said to follow you with their eyes without ever moving their heads!

Owl, Screech
Otus asio and Otus kennicottii 8 1/2"

Formerly, they were one species and are now the Eastern and Western Screech Owls with voice and range differences. The Eastern one has two color phases, reddish-brown and gray while

149

the Western race is gray to dark brown. They are really mis-named as their call is a soft trill. In some places the call of this bird was said to mean death. They were said to be able to turn themselves into witches and the reverse and sucked blood out of infants. As a result, they were nailed to doors to avert evil and were the death Owl in Florida. The Winnebago and the Eastern Cherokee said that one hooting near a lodge meant that someone would die. The Penobscot said that if you mocked one of these birds, it would burn up your house. The Pueblo claimed that they were either very violent or so gentle that you could pick one up. In the southern states if you were on a journey and heard one hoot, you had better go home. If you were a Cajun of Bayou la Fouche in Louisiana, you would get out of bed on hearing this owl call and turn your left shoe upside down! The Mayan had a calendar of nineteen gods in a religious year. One of them was the Moan Bird or Screech Owl who was associated with the War God and God of Death, called Ah Puch.

Owl, Short-eared
Otus flammeus 13-17"

These birds are circumpolar in the Northern Hemisphere and are found on some Oceanic Islands and into South America. Their plumage is tawny in color with bold streaking on the breast and lighter on the belly. These ground nesting birds have ear tufts that are barely visible.

This bird fared better than the Screech Owl. The Ainu of Japan said that if the bird looked at you all was well. If he looked away or at you with half-closed eyes, it meant that something was wrong with you! It was a popular bird in England and other places where voles erupted in great numbers. Suddenly, this Owl would turn up and take care of the problem. The Alaskan Inuit said that its beak was small because once it was a little girl in the Yukon who was changed by magic into a bird with a long bill. She became frightened and sprung up flying erratically and hit the side of a house. This flattened her beak and face so it has been that way ever since. They are often seen by day in the open country.

Owl, Snowy *Nyctea scandiaca 24"*

It is a large uncommon diurnal Owl of the Arctic regions. It is white with a little barring, has a big head and very yellow eyes. Lemmings are their main food and if it is a bad year then these birds will wander further south. The earliest record that we have of this bird is that of two birds in the cave paintings at Trois-Freres. This makes one wonder if they ate them as the Inuit did. In the North, these birds are said to have greater prophetic powers than any other bird.

According to the Greenland Inuit, it was this bird who changed the Raven from white to black. These two birds were once great friends. The Raven made a black and white dress for the Owl (its summer plumage), while the Owl made a pair of whalebone boots and a white dress for the Raven. However, the Raven would not stay still long enough for the Owl to try them on. The Owl got annoyed and said that he would pour lamp oil on him if he did not stay still. Well, he did not, so the Owl covered him with sooty lamp oil and he has been black ever since.

A California tribe said that if the "Great White Owl" landed near their village, it was either for a life or for money. The headsman would hold a conference and usually it was decided on money not a tribesman. The chief would then put on Owl feathers and take money and in a solemn ceremony, would toss it into the air beneath the Owl. Some tribes thought that the heart of the Snowy Owl, when taken into battle, had the power to encourage men, avert danger and find success. The Micmac of New Brunswick said that its call was Raven-like and sorrowful because the bird was unhappy that the "golden age" had gone and now all the animals quarreled!

Oxpecker *Buphagus 8 1/2"*

This name is from the French "pique-boeuf." These two odd Starlings of Southern Africa are adapted to live with animals. They fly around in flocks and settle on the backs of cattle looking for insects and ticks that infest these beasts. The cattle seem to like this but some Africans claimed that these birds warned their animal hosts of danger by flying up with rattling noises. They are popular with photographers who like the pictures they make. Farmers liked them too but not so cattlemen. They are against these birds as they claim that they keep the tick wounds open so as to drink the blood. It is known that these birds do not like tick-free animals as much as those loaded with them.

Oystercatcher *Haematopus ostralegus 17"*

These are the large conspicuous noisy Plover-like birds of the open beaches and rocky coasts around the world. They have a long blunt vertically flattened bill which is a powerful tool with which to chisel off limpets, oysters, mussels and clams. There was an old Gaelic tradition that said this bird covered Jesus with seaweed when he was being pursued as this bird knew that it was not yet time for his death. The bird was blessed with the form of a cross on his back when he flies. The Gaels in Scotland called it "St. Bride's Bird." This is because when the saint visited one of the northern islands, he carried this black and white Oystercatcher in both hands.

Parrots in general

The word Parrot comes from the French "perrot" while Parakeet comes from Little Peter. Parrots are not found in Egyptian art or in the Bible. These birds appeal to people because of their bright colors, are easily tamed, can imitate human voices, show affection to each other, are long-lived and use their feet like hands. Forget the fact that their voices can be very strident and their chatter endless.

There are 315 species, ranging from the three and a half inch Pigmy of the Papuan regions to the forty inch gaudy long-tailed Macaws of the Amazon jungle. They have large heads, strong down-curved beaks, short necks and have two toes going forward and two backwards.

By the time of Alexander the Great, Parrots had arrived in Greece from India and Persia and were carried at Ptolemy's procession at Alexandria. Pliny told of a Parrot who learned many words including "Hail Caesar." He also said that when they got drunk, they became lascivious! The early bestiarists said that they hated rain as their colors ran. They probably confused them with the African Turaco which has crimson pigment in its feathers that is water soluble. People used to claim that a Parrot's beak was so hard that if you threw it from a height, it would save itself by landing on its tightly closed beak which broke the shock. They were said to be taught how to talk before the age of two years.

In ancient times, they were kept in cages of ivory, tortoise shell and silver and were fed almonds, nuts and poppy seeds. As

Parrot

a result, they were considered a delicacy and one Roman Emperor even fed them to his Lions. In Tudor England, they were kept in cages that were carved and painted and closed with a silver pin. They even decorated them with mirrors and fresh flowers. Madame Pompadour went as far as to give her Parrots their food and drink in the best porcelains.

A Parrot is among the famous dead in Westminster Abbey. It is next to the effigy of Frances Theresa, the Duchess of Richmond, who is dressed in the robe worn at the Coronation of Queen Anne. Her Parrot apparently died of grief a few days after his mistress so was placed next to her.

The German explorer Humboldt told of his journeys to South America and how he met up with an ancient Parrot who had the sole knowledge of a dead language. It was of the extinct Atute. In the Far East, Parrots were said to be tattlers of the doings of wives. In minor castes of Northern India, these birds served as a marriage totem and were sacred. Images of them were carved out of cotton wood or made of clay and hung in the marriage shed. If a Parrot was born the same day as a child, it became its soul bird.

Here is a great tale. The Maharajah of Nawanager was said to have had a Parrot that was one hundred and fifteen years old. This ancient bird traveled around in a Rolls Royce and had an international passport so that he could accompany his master anywhere!

Parrot, African Gray *Psittacus erithacus 13"*

This bird can be found in literature since the Greek and Roman times. It was and still is esteemed for its talking and imitating abilities. It is one of the most costly. In its native West Africa, this red-tailed gray bird does a lot of harm to the crops.

King George V of England, had one that he called Charlotte. He obtained it while a midshipman in Port Said. This bird remained close to him all his life. She viewed documents from the king's shoulder and occasionally would say, "What about it?" When the royal vessel Britannia was at Cowes, this sea-loving Parrot would say, "Where's the Captain?" When the king fell ill, she kept calling, "Where's the Captain? When the king was feeling better, the bird was allowed to see him. She alighted on his shoulder and said, "Bless my buttons, bless my buttons, all is well!"

Cockatoo, White *Cacatua alba 18"*

In the Austra-Malaysan area, there are sixteen species of these mainly white birds. These Cockatoos differ from other Parrots in having a crest of long pointed feathers that they can raise or lower at will. Some have color. In New Guinea, these feathers were used by the natives in headdresses. Many of these birds were purchased from the natives as pets. A Seabee outfit on the Solomon Islands in World War II obtained one. They taught it to

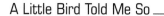

constantly say "Bledsoe said so." This was to annoy the arrogant officer named Bledsoe!

Macaws

There are fifteen species of these gaudily plumaged birds who live in the tropical rain forests from Mexico to South America. The two most commonly seen are the Blue and Yellow and the Red and Green. They commanded great prices as they were very popular as pets. There was and is much illegal traffic in Parrots and it is being stopped as best possible. The feathers of these birds make great salmon flies. Their feathers were used in many Native American ceremonies and ranked with the Turkey and the Eagle in importance. Not being native to the United States, the natives had to go south to find them and also pick up much needed salt.

Parakeet, Carolina
Conuropis carolinensis 12"

This now extinct bird ranged from North Dakota to Florida in the early nineteenth century. They inhabited heavily forested areas. When the trees were cut and replaced with fruit trees and grain, it was the beginning of the end for our only native Parrot. They were slaughtered for sport and to control their predation on the fruit and grain crops. They had a habit of hovering over the dead birds so they became an easy target. They became rare by 1900 and the last was seen in the Everglades over eighty years ago. Mark Catesby, who wrote on the Birds of the Carolinas said, "it's guts were a certain and speedy poison to cats."

Partridge, Gray *Perdix perdix 12"*

This name comes from the Latin "perdix" and the Old English "pertriche" and the Scottish "patrick." This bird and the Chukkar Partridge *Alectoris chukkar* 13" are often confused with each other. The Bohemians said that a flight of these birds over your house meant that it would burn up. Aldrovanus said that tame birds would cry if poison was being prepared in the house! Men were said to die more easily when lying on a bed of Partridge wings. Both St. Jerome and St. Augustine said that the devil could take the form of one of these birds. They were generally thought of as disgusting, cunning and sensuous and this can be seen in some tapestries done in the Middle Ages.

These birds were said to have amazing procreative abilities. All the female had to do was to stand near the male when the wind was blowing, or if he flew over her head and she heard his voice, she became impregnated. She was supposed to hide her eggs from her mate and even steal others. However, on hatching the young would go back to their real parents allegorizing evil turned to good!

The Gray Partridge and the Chukkar have been successfully introduced into this country at various places in the Middle West where they are known as "The Hun or Hungarian Partridge."

The carol "On the first day of Christmas, my true love sent to me," etc., of the Victorian age covers the twelve days between Christmas and Epiphany. Note: Partridges do not usually sit in pear trees and the pear tree is a phallic symbol! So much for this good eating bird.

Peacock and Peafowl
Pavo cristatus 86-92"

These names come from the Latin "pavo" and the Anglo-Saxon "pawe." They were first domesticated in India and Ceylon, their homelands. They were taken by Phoenician traders to Egypt before the time of Solomon. It was Alexander the Great who introduced them to Greece. The Peacock was the favorite bird of Juno. When an empress died, one was liberated over her funeral pyre, just like the Eagle being liberated at the emperor's funeral. This was to show that they were immortal. The Greeks had severe punishments for harming one and there was a Peacock zoo in Athens in the fifth century. Peacock tail feathers, in pagan times, stood for the stars in the heaven or Argus whose 101 eyes at his death were transferred by Juno to her Peacock. The Romans fattened them up as a delicacy and cooked them as a most exotic dish. Cleopatra was said to have worn a few Peacock feathers as a state robe (and maybe something else as well).

In China and Japan, there was a legend on the use of their plumes as a symbol of rank. It was said that a defeated general hid in a forest where there were many Peacocks. When the enemy arrived all they saw were these quiet birds so assumed no one was there. The general escaped and became the ancestor of five kings. When they came to power, they instituted the conferring of the Peacock feathers as a reward for bravery. In the eighth century A.D. in China, districts paid tribute in Peacocks since they were needed in imperial processions and to be given to military and civil officials for their faithful services. The feathers were given according to the honor to be received. There were the "flower" feather, "green" feather, "one-eyed," "two-eyed" or "three-eyed" feathers. The white or albino Peacock was an object of worship. In oriental art, the Peacock and the peony frequently were seen together.

In the jungles of Southeast Asia, it was said that these birds warned the villagers of tigers, leopards or big snakes by their harsh cries so were considered birds of magic. The Hindu said that these birds had angel feathers, a thief's walk and the devil's voice—a very good definition. The notion that their tail feathers had "evil eyes" originated in Egypt. They thought that if a young person was ill or dying, it was because there were Peacock feathers in the house. Keeping them outside carried no evil.

When the Pope was carried in his processional chair at Easter, two chamberlains carried a "flabetti" which was a fan of Ostrich plumes, tipped with Peacock feathers and mounted on a long pole. Aside from being a good insect repellent, it symbolized the all-seeing eye of the church with its power and immortality. As Peacocks were Oriental in origin, early Christians tried to subdue all pagan thoughts. They fostered the idea that these birds molted so beautifully that they symbolized immortality. In the early Christian catacombs, there are carved Peacocks facing one another, standing for the soul of the departed and drinking of the fountain of life. St. Augustine experimented with these birds and claimed that their flesh never decayed and who but the Creator made them that way.

Other faiths used these feathers in different ways. The "Peacock Throne" formerly used by the kings in Delhi India, and then by the shahs of Persia was so called as it was fanned and studded with jewels. In India, it was sacred to many people and in Punjab its smoked feathers were said to heal snakebites. Its mating time comes at the rainy season, thus it was claimed to carry a charm under its wing and swallowed its excrement so that it could not be used for medicines.

At the time of Francis the First, Peacocks were used as a table decoration but not eaten. The skin was stripped and the body prepared with spices and sewed up again to make it last a long time. For wedding feasts, its bill and throat would be filled with cotton and camphor and then lit for amusement. Their heads were used as ornaments by the ancient English kings. Oaths were sworn on Peacocks at the time of Edward the First. They were looked upon as a royal bird and eaten only by them and not the common man. They were roasted and covered with pastry and the feathers put back in the crust. In 1550, this is how you cooked a Peacock: "A Peacock flayed, parboiled, larded and stuck with cloves, roasted, with its feet wrapped to keep them from scorching, then covered again with its own skin as soon as he was cold and so underpropped that, as alive, he seems to stand on his legs."

In heraldry, he was depicted with his train erect to signify that "he is in his pride." The proverb "let him keep peacock to himself" meant do not inflict your oddities on others and was the symbol of pride. From Aesop comes the thought "It is not only fine feathers that makes a fine bird!"

Pelicans 45-65"

There are six species of Pelicans, two of which are in the United States. They are large aquatic, fish-eating birds with huge bills and throat pouches and webbed toes. Some form of its name is found in many European languages. The Spaniards and Portuguese called it "Alcatraz" from the Arabic word for bucket referring to its pouch.

Alcatraz Island in San Francisco Bay, was named by the early Spanish explorers as Pelicans used to nest there. The Seri Tribe of the Tiburon Islands in the Gulf of California ascribed the creation of the world to the Pelican. They said that he first raised the earth above the primeval waters. One of their customs was to tie a broken-winged bird to a stake near the seashore and then appropriate the fishes brought to it by the other Pelicans.

In early Christian literature, the Pelican symbolized the suffering of Christ on the Cross. When St. Jerome translated the Bible, he said in Psalm 102 "I am the Pelican of the wilderness." This was a real misnomer as the word "apelekon" was the Greek for any bird pecking wood like an axe such as the Woodpecker. No way could a Pelican do that! St. Jerome went on to say that those dead in sin were made new again by the blood of Christ. They believed that the Pelican laid her eggs, hatched them and when the young were a few days old, they hit the parents who in turn killed them. Three days later the mother pierced her breast and out came blood which the young drank and so were revived. This was the proof that St. Jerome was correct. In heraldry, plays, poetry and symbolism, the Pelican was pictured on its nest with its beak tearing at its breast and was known as "The Pelican in her Piety." This was based on the fact that the European White Pelican often rests its beak on its breast like other Pelicans do. These birds get a reddish-pink tinge on the breast from the oil sac excretion during courtship and mating. The more they preen, the rosier the breast. Added to this, is the fact that the inside of the bill is reddish and they regurgitate their food to feed their young. The Resurrection fitted easily into this early religious dogma and the notion persisted. St. Jerome said that it was the male who restored life to the young while St. Augustine said it was the female!

In Hamlet, William Shakespeare did not care which one did it when he said: "To his good friends thus wide, I'll open my arms like the kind life-rendering Pelican repast them with my blood." The Pelican in its piety is found in stone, wood and glass in churches, cathedrals and schools, and became the symbol of the Reformation. The Sacrament is reserved in the Durham

Cathedral, England, in a silver Pelican over the altar. The most famous use of the Pelican in this country is at St. James Church, Goose Creek, South Carolina, where the Pelican replaces the cross outside the church. It is found over the entrance door. The present building dates from 1714-1719 but the Pelican crumbled and had to be replaced in 1907. The first minister assigned to the church was from the Society for the Preservation of the Gospel and their emblem was the Pelican.

Most people think of this bird in the jolly jingles of "what a wonderful bird is the Pelican, his beak holds more than his belly can" and "holds in his beak enough for a week." This is really not true as they keep their food in their beaks just long enough to drain out the water and then they swallow the fish. The pouch is really a big dip net!

Penguins 16-48"

The fifteen species of Penguins get their name from two Welsh words meaning white head plus the Greek "speniskos" meaning a small wedge which refers to their narrow flipper-like wings. They use these for swimming and not for flying which they are unable to do. The name Penguin was first applied to the now extinct Great Auk, a totally unrelated bird. Penguins and Auks, both black and white in plumage, got all mixed up in early literature. Penguins get as far north as the equator but live mainly in colder climes while the Auks are very northern birds.

The Dutch navigator DeWert in 1559 had to live on Penguins to survive to get him back home again. Pretty fishy meals! These birds used to be referred to as "Magellanic Geese." Penguins are a very old primitive group with feathers closely packed all over the body and not in feather tracts like other birds. This forms a

Penguins

thick mass with a shiny surface that is water repellent so these birds are especially well suited for marine living. Once the Australian government leased an island full of Penguins to a concern who reduced these birds to oil. The oil was more salable than the whole bird! The concern did a good job of trying to destroy the population before it was stopped.

Penguin, Jackass *Spheniscus demersus 28"*

These birds live off South Africa and have had a bad time with many oil spills in that region. The name comes from its habit of throwing back its head and emitting a strange noise that sounds like the braying of an ass!

Penguin, Macaroni
Eudyptes chrysolophus 24"

These southern circumpolar birds probably got their odd name at the time when the word "macaroni" stood for a fop or exquisite hair fashion, the reason being that they have very conspicuous plumes of golden-yellow feathers on either side of the head!

Petrels *6-10"*

These dark colored birds with white rumps are commonly seen following ships in the oceans of the world. The name Petrel comes from "pitterals or runners of the sea" and from St. Peter's trying to walk on the Sea of Galilee. They became known as "Little Peters." The Italian sailors thought that they must be in the special care of Christ's mother, Madra Cara, their patroness. The name became anglicized to "Mother Cary's Chickens" and "Mother Caru," a sea witch good at raising the wind and a cousin of Davey Jones! The French called them "Oiseau de Notre Dame" or "Aves Sanctae." They got these names because of their so-called ability to walk upon the waters with their legs hanging down and feet seemingly touching the water as they searched for food. No sailor would harm one as some thought that they were the living form of the souls of drowned comrades. In Brittany, they were said to be the captains who mistreated their crews so were condemned to flutter over the water as Storm Petrels. Others, said that they were the souls of drowned mariners seeking prayers from the living. The skeptics said that they were devil birds fluttering over the corpses of the lost. It is no wonder that no one would hurt one of these birds!

Pheasant, Great Argus
Argusianus argus 72"

This bird has gray-brown plumage with secondary flight feathers elongated down the center of it back with a series of eye-spots, hence its name. These speckled feathers were used by only the men in their native Sumatra, Celebes and Borneo. In the Malays, around the time of King Solomon, this bird was dowdy in color and asked the white Crow to paint his feathers. This the Crow did and when he asked the Pheasant to paint him, he refused and threw ink on the Crow.

Pheasant, Ring-necked
Phasianus colchicus male 35" female 21"

This bird originally inhabited Asia Minor as far as China. There is a fairly well documented legend that says the original birds were brought to Greece in 1300 B.C. They were supposed to have been brought there by Jason and the Argonauts who may have sailed to Colchis to get the Golden Fleece. The name "Phasianus" comes from the River Phasis (Rion) in Georgia at the end of the Black Sea. The site was Colchis, so Linnaeus, the Father of modern taxonomy, called the bird after its native country and the river where it was found - *Phasianus colchicus*. When they arrived in Europe, they were called the "Phasian Bird" from the land of Colchis.

The Greeks and Romans kept them in pens and eventually took them to England. Many escaped and multiplied, and used to be taken in the wild by snares, nets, crossbows and by falconry. This all changed with the advent of firearms. Henry the Eighth had a French priest on his payroll called the "Fesseunt

165

Breeder." At the time of Edward the First, these birds were considered a royal bird and oaths were sworn upon them (likewise Swans, Peacocks, and Herons). In ancient China, they were regarded as Thunderbirds because of the noise made by the beating of their wings. They were even said to beat drums with their wings to make thunder. In the spring, young couples would dance to bring on rain and imitate the beating of the wings of this bird. The male is the gaudiest with a long ornate tail. The birds we see today are hybrids of forty or more types and vary considerably in color. An ancient authority on food claimed that this bird "is said to have wholesome and nutritious food." How true!

Phoebe, Eastern *Sayornis phoebe 7"*

Its name and call are the same! This gray tail-wagger of the Flycatcher family was probably the first bird ever banded in America. John James Audubon, in 1803 in Pennsylvania, tied silver threads to four young birds that he found in a nest. Two of these birds returned to him the next year. They go south when the insect population gets low and come back again in the spring when the food supply is adequate. They are usually one of the earliest birds to come north again.

Phoenix

This is the bird that is not a bird but a myth. It was said to have been first described by Herodotus and associated with fire. When it got old, after five hundred years, it flew to the Lebanon Mountains and filled its wings with fragrant herbs. Then it flew to Heliopolis to the Temple of the Sun and there burned itself up. The next day, from its bones appeared a sweet smelling worm.

On the second day, it became a bird and on the third it was a perfect Phoenix. It adapted itself readily to early Christianity with such symbols as Christ, the Resurrection, immortality, the Trinity and the penitent sinner!

In the Egyptian religion, it gained a place as a god. It symbolized the sun which burns itself to death each evening and is resurrected again each morning. Some people thought that the large Argus Pheasant may have been the origin of the Egyptian legend. The same story was told among the ancient Chinese. Some people thought that it was red like the flame from which it came. The Phoenix even became the symbol of kingship in the royal courts of France and England!

Pigeon also see Dove

In this family there are 289 species of varying sizes, shapes, colors and habits. The birds vary from the 7" Ground Dove of lower North America and well into South America; to the 33" beautiful Blue-Crowned Pigeon of New Guinea and the extinct Dodo. They are all stout-bodied and small-headed with short bills that are thickened at the end. They feed their young on "Pigeon milk" which is comparable to mammal's milk. It is the lining of the crop that sloughs off and is like a cheese curd. In order to get it, the young have to put their bills into that of the parent's.

The word Pigeon comes from the Latin word "pipre" or to peep. Christopher Columbus's real name was Colombo meaning pigeon. The dovecote was invented to keep out predators and divided into small apartments for Pigeons to use for nesting. The word "pigeonhole" is now used to mean desks and storage areas and is derived from dovecote. The thousands of Pigeons in St. Mark's Square in Venice will no longer bother visitors as they are going to be trapped and killed as a health hazard. Some 30% of the 5000 or so birds have a form of salmonella that can be transferred to humans.

Pigeon, Passenger
Ecopistes migratorius 17"

This now extinct bird once numbered in the billions. They nested in unbelievably huge flocks in the forests of the Midwest and Canada. Alexander Wilson, in 1810, said he saw a flock of two billion while Mark Catesby said that they were so numerous that they had to roost on each other's backs. They were said to darken the skies in flight and their wings sounded like gales. *Ecopistes* is Greek for wanderer. The Native Americans dried and smoked the adult birds and boiled the squabs (young) for oil.

However, it was the greedy White Men who were the culprits. They shot them, trapped them in their nests, clubbed them to death and even chopped down trees to get to the young. In 1850, a railroad employed 1000 people who did nothing else but catch and market these birds. In 1855, a New York handler had daily a turnover of 18,000 birds. In 1869, seven and a half million were taken from one area. The feathers were used for bedding, the fat for butter and the birds preserved in salt. Their blood was a cure for eye disorders and their gizzards were dried and used in gallstone attacks. In order to nest, these birds needed the stimulus of several thousand individuals and the last great nesting colony was destroyed in Michigan in 1878. Martha, the last Passenger Pigeon died in the Cincinnati Zoo in 1914.

In New York, the Seneca called these birds "Jah 'Jowa" meaning "big bread." They closed their schools for several weeks in the spring so the students could help their elders harvest maple syrup and these birds for their larders. In Ontario Canada, there was a "rhyme" that went as follows: "When I shoot my rifle clear at Pigeons in the sky, I'll say good-bye to pork and beans and live on Pigeon pie." These birds made ecclesiastical history when, in 1867, the Bishop of Montreal, Canada, exorcised them with Holy Water as if they were demons because they ate too much local grain!

Pigeon, Wood *Columba palumbus 16"*

This common widespread European bird has a sort of complaining love note. John Watters in his "Birds of Ireland" wrote of how it was said that a dove was perched in the neighborhood of the Holy Cross when the Redeemer was expiring, wailing its notes of sorrow, and kept repeating the words "kyrie, kyrie eleison" - "Lord have mercy" so as to alleviate the agony of his dying moments. He had a good imagination. It was believed that the direction from which you heard it call could be good or evil and this call can be pretty noisy. They are often called "Ring Dove" from the broad white band across the wings and white markings on either side of the neck. The monarchs of Great Britain had a decoy maker who carved life-sized wooden copies of this large good eating bird so that they could be shot over.

The expression "stool-pigeon" meant a decoy who betrayed the flock and "pigeon-livered" meant a coward.

Pitta *6-11"*

These small plump birds with stout bills, big heads, short necks, long legs and feet and practically no tail are very odd looking. However, they possess the most marvelous colors in their plumages. These very loose-webbed feathers come in green, blue, purple, red and yellow with several of these colors on each

169

species. The twenty-three species live on the floors and lower levels of the wet tropical forests from Asia to Malaysia, Australia and some Pacific Islands. They seem to have no close relatives but the noisy Pitta of Australia is known as the "Dragon Bird!"

Plover 6-12"

The word Plover comes from the Latin "pluvia" meaning rain. The Germans called them "Regenpfeifer" or rain sandpipers but they have no connection with rain. The thirty-eight species of this bird can be found all over the portion of the world that is ice free. They are plump birds with a Pigeon-like bill that has a swollen tip. "Charadrius" was a Plover with unusual prophetic gifts. For example, if someone was seriously ill, the Plover would come and look at the person. If it was a critical situation or death was imminent, the Plover would look away. However, if he stared at the patient and the patient stared back, then all who had come to mourn could celebrate instead. The Plover was one of King Solomon's favorite birds. Being a water bird, it would head for the watering places in the desert. The king, being wise, once followed this bird and was led to the Queen of Sheba. Other birds did the same for the famous pair!

Plover, Black-bellied
Pluvialis squatorala 11 1/2"

They are called "Christmas Plover" in Florida as that is when they arrive there for the winter. Then they look rather dull, but in the spring they turn a lovely black with their backs barred with light gray. They are often called "Bottle-head" from their large round heads.

Plover, Golden *Pluvialis 11 1/2"*

These black birds with golden spots on their backs breed in the high north and winter in the tropics, looking drab like their cousin the Black-bellied Plover. The Eurasian species *apricaria* were known in the Middle Ages as the "Seven whistlers" and, when heard at night, they foretold of harm. They were said to be the souls of the Jews who took part in the Crucifixion and so were condemned to wander forever. In Shropshire, England, they said of these seven that six were flying around looking for the seventh, and when they found that bird, it would be the end of the world.

The American Golden Plover *Pluvialis dominica* does a loop migration. They breed in the far north, and the east coast birds go to Labrador in the fall and fill up on berries. Then they head for Argentina, 2400 miles away, using up less than two ounces of body fat for the one-way trip. They do it in about forty-eight hours. Going north in the spring, they take a route of eight thousand miles via the Mississippi River for better weather, more food and no fog. The first year birds are on their own and go south via the Mississippi by themselves so getting two summers in the first year of their lives with no parental guidance.

Plover, Killdeer
Charadrius vociferus 10 1/2"

This New World bird has a thick neck, a double black collar, golden-rust rump and is plump looking. Like all Plovers, their bill is Pigeon-like with a swelling at the tip. They run in short starts and stops, love golf courses and open gravel areas where they nest. They can be very noisy with their "killdee or dee, dee, dee." The Pueblo said that they were the leaders of the dancers

171

and protectors of water holes. They guard and protect their young by using the "broken wing act." They sort of drag one wing along the ground, calling loudly to lure people and other predators away from the nest or young. The Zuni said that anyone could wear its feathers; but, if you break up a nest, you will soon have a broken arm or leg. Many farmers believe that when you hear them call in the spring, then it is time to get planting.

Poorwill *Phalaenoptilus nuttallii 8"*

This bird is the smallest of the Nightjar family. They live in the Middle and Western parts of the United States. They can be told from the Nighthawk by a short rounded tail and wings lacking white. They nicely call their name. All the birds in this family are cryptically colored gray and brown to match their surroundings. There is a question as to whether these birds migrate or hibernate in the winter. Some birds have been found in crevices of canyon walls with a temperature of 65 degrees instead of the usual 102 for birds. Their breathing was slow and their digestive processes had stopped. To the Pueblo, these birds were the symbol of sleep as they were never seen by day!

Ptarmigan *15"*

There are four species of boreal Grouse and all have feathered toes and tarsus. All but the Red Grouse *Lapopus lagopus* of Great Britain and Ireland acquire three molts a year. In winter they are white, in the fall and spring they are mottled, and in the summer they are reddish brown to blend in with their surroundings.

The Native Americans said that they learned about Snowshoes from these birds. The birds grow spurs on their toes so that they walk easier on snow and do not fall in. The Icelanders had a myth that said that the Virgin Mary required all birds to walk through fire and only the Ptarmigan refused. While he kept his feathered legs, he was condemned to be timid and to be the prey of the Hawk but was allowed to molt into white feathers in the winter for protection. They are Alaska's state bird.

Puffin *Fratercula arctica 12"*

These chunky bodied, large headed small seabirds got their name from their puffed out look. They are the best walkers in the Alcid or Auk family as they have a comic waddle instead of a shuffle. In the Gaspe, where many nest, they are called

Puffin

"Sea-parrots" because of their big, thick colored bills. The red, yellow and gray colors of their bills are on the flag of Ecuador even though these birds live in the Northern Hemisphere — just a coincidence! Their bills become duller in winter as they shed the outer lining that covers them. In Cornwall, England, they claimed that King Arthur was turned into one on death. Three hundred of these birds were used by an abbot to lease the Scilly Isles from King Edward III of England. In 1337, three Puffins were worth a penny! Puffins were allowed to be eaten on feast days and during Lent by the Church of Rome. The Church Fathers obviously stretched their consciences by saying that while they looked like birds they tasted like fish. A comment recorded in 1673 tells of the bad taste of these fish-eating birds and how they were fit only for servants to eat!

Puffin, Horned and Tufted
Fratercula cornicula and Fratercula cirrhata 15"

These birds are both Northern Pacific species. The Horned Puffin has a fleshy "horn" extending up from the eye which is hard to see. The Tufted Puffin has pale yellow head tufts going over the back of the neck. In Kodiak, Alaska, people made rattles out of the beaks of these birds and used them in ceremonies. They were also said to be used by witches to call up a storm.

Quail Coturnix coturnix 8"

The word Quail comes from the Dutch "quakel" and the English "quale" meaning to croak. The Coturnix is a Robin-sized Quail. The most famous flight of these birds is recorded in Exodus 13 as having saved the lives of the Israelites on the plains of Sinai. It is now estimated that several million of these migrating birds were killed in one night and two days. They have been netted since at least the 23rd century B.C. and they can still be seen on wall scenes.

The Greeks and Romans kept them for fights and esteemed them for their courage. In China, these birds were carried in bags hanging from men's girdles and were treated with great care. The owner would blow on a reed to arouse the birds to fight. Next, little millet was thrown into the ring and the fight would start. The Japanese also used them in fights, domesticated them and kept them in cages. They used them as egg producers. They discovered that a bird could lay up to two hundred eggs a year. This made them often more plentiful in the markets than Hen's eggs. They were the symbol of poverty as their flecked feathers looked like rags or patched clothing.

These birds migrated in amazing numbers until the 19th and 20th centuries when they were slaughtered and sent to market. The Egyptians exported three million in 1920 and by 1930 all the big flocks had gone. In ancient times, the Bishops of Capri got a large part of their wealth from a tax on the many migrating Quail. The birds were said to be stupid and easy to catch. When these birds returned to Europe in the spring, it meant better weather but the birds were better eating in the fall! A 1542 note on food said, "Quail do not nourish much because they give sad humors." Pliny went as far as to say that there were so many of them migrating that they would settle on the sails of ships and their weight even sank some.

Quail, Bobwhite *Colinus virginianus 9 1/2"*

These round looking birds of the New World live in the eastern sections of the country. They are a mottled red-brown with a gray tail. The male sports a white throat and the female a buff colored one. They are ground nesters with precocial young who can run shortly after hatching. They stay together in large groups and roost on the ground in a circle. They do this tail to tail so they can take off at top speed in an emergency and never collide. The distinctive call of this bird, who says his name, was used in the Native American wars as a means of communicating. The Winnebago called them "Whistle-birds." In the south of the United States there is a saying that if a pair of these birds crossed your path on you way to conclude a bargain, you had better go home and abandon the idea.

Quail, California and Gambel's Quail
Callipella californica and Callipella gambelii 11"

Both these Western North American Quail have black faces and throats with gray chests and prominent teardrop plumes on top of their heads. The Gambel's has a white belly and chestnut sides. The California species has scaled underparts and brown sides streaked with white. The Gambel's replaces the California in desert areas of California, British Columbia down to Baja California, and hybridize where they meet. Their prominent head plumes were used by various Native American tribes for ceremonial and ornamental affairs.

Quail, Scaled Callipella squamata 10"

These are birds of the semi-desert scrublands of the Southwestern United States going into Mexico. They are grayish with dark tipped feathers that give them a scaled appearance with a white tipped crown. The Native Americans said that these birds were so secretive that it was taboo to use them in any ceremonies or offerings. They considered them improper message bearers!

Quetzal, Resplendent
Pharomachus mocino 14"

These are one of the most brilliantly colored birds and are found in the highlands of Southern Mexico and Costa Rica where they live in the rain forests. Their plumage is a bronze-green with red and white underparts. The four upper tail coverts of the male grow into long shimmering green plumes with the two central ones adding about two more feet giving it the look of a big bird. Their plumage is soft and loose on very thin skin. Their feathered legs end in weak feet. They have yoke-toes, two going forward and the other two backwards like Parrots, Cuckoos, Toucans and Woodpeckers. The exception here is that the second toe is shifted to the rear and not the fourth, and the first two are joined together at the base.

Before the Aztec in Central America, the Toltecs associated this Trogon with spring because of its lovely feathers. It became their symbol of life and creation. They also associated it with the serpent, a symbol of death. "Quetzalcoatl" was a plumed serpent, an anthropomorphic god with white skin, a black beard made from Quetzal feathers and had its long plumes in his hair. The Aztec and Mayan adopted "Quetzalcoatl" who they believed lived under the earth where happy souls rested. He was biding his time to return to earth. When Hernando Cortez reached Mexico in his ships, the natives thought that "Quetzalcoatl" had returned. Cortez smartly put Quetzal feathers in his helmet and this superstition may have helped the Spanish conquer the Aztec empire.

The Aztec and Mayan people felt that the Quetzal was an object of worship and the spiritual protection of tribal chiefs escorting men into battle. It was also their God of the Air so its feathers were woven into their tapestries. They never killed one; they just plucked the feathers and then released the birds so that they could grow new feathers again. Montezuma wore a cloak made of these beautiful feathers. In 1825, when Guatemala separated from Mexico, they took this bird as a natural symbol representing the best legends in their history and hope for the future. Their monetary unit is a quetzal. These birds are often portrayed on their postage stamps, coins and is on their state flag.

The Mayan have a nice story of how the god who made all of the creatures had a few scraps left over so he made the Hummingbird. The only problem was that he was dull colored. The Quetzal then very kindly gave him some of his lovely feathers. They also thought that if you kept a Quetzal in captivity, he would die of a broken heart. An even better tale is that of how when making a nest the birds would make two entrances, so when the male finished his share of the incubating he could get out without hurting his long train of feathers. So much for myths!

Rail, Sora *Porzana carolina 9"*

All Rails are soberly and cryptically colored with stout legs so they can walk in their natural habitat, the marsh. There are two types; The long-billed ones and the short-billed ones, such as the Sora. In Europe they are called Crakes.

From the Latin "rallus" and the French "reille" we get our word Rail. These birds have always been known as a good game bird - now protected. In Florida, they call them "Ortolon." This is the name of a gastromically noted European Finch but has been transferred to numerous species as excellent birds for the table. The saying "thin as a Rail" originally referred to the avian Rail and not to the wooden or steel type of fence rail.

Raven *Corvus corax 26"*

The Raven is the largest and most widespread of the Crow family. They are black with a long heavy bill and a wedge-shaped tail. Their voice is harsh and often ends in a long, drawn out croak. In flight, they glide and flap their wings, resembling Hawks. They are more solitary and a lot larger than a Crow. In literature and myths, these two birds are often confused. Generally speaking, the message is that black feathers means a black character even though these birds were once thought to be white! The French had an interesting theory that bad priests were turned into Ravens and bad nuns were turned into Crows. There are Arabic and Jewish legends that say that Noah first let the Raven out of the Ark to see what happened to the waters. The Raven found some floating carrion and so never returned. Noah then cursed him and said from henceforth their food would be carrion and their flight would be crooked.

The Raven seems to be either good or bad but mainly the latter. It was a good bird in helping several saints. One bird was said to have brought bread each day to St. Paul the Hermit, for sixty days. The day before he died, the bird brought double the amount as St. Anthony was visiting. St. Benedict's life was saved by a Raven who took away a loaf of poisoned bread sent to the saint by a jealous priest. St. Vincent was tortured to death at Saragossa and his body was thrown to the wild beasts. The Ravens came and took away his body to his brothers at Valencia. There he rested in a tomb until the Christians were displaced by the Moors. The remains of the saint were carried by the exiled monks to a place called St. Vincent where he was buried and watched over by Ravens. These birds were said to have given noble services to St. Meinrod, St. Oswald, St. Francis, St. Ida and others. They fed Elijah the Tishbite, while he was hiding from King Ahab according to the First Book of Kings. The Greeks and the Romans said that the Raven was a God of omens so they put his effigy on their banners and followed his auguries. The Roman champion Valerus defeated a Gaul because a Raven was sitting on his helmet and struck the Gaul with his beak and wings. The Raven was the sacred bird of the Druids and later became an old Anglo-Saxon emblem. The Bayeaux tapestries show William the Conquerer under the banner of a Raven at the Battle of Hastings. The Danish kings put him on their flags. Odin, the Norse God, had a black and a white one. They were known as Hugin and Munin, mind and memory. The god sent them off each morning and they returned each evening with all the news. If it was unusual then Odin, in Raven guise, flew out to investigate. The Norsemen took them on their journeys and liberated them as guides to be followed. The birds would return if there was no land around. If they did not come back, it assumed that land was ahead. Iceland and Greenland were said to have been found that way!

There is a strange tale from Cornwall, Wales and Brittany about King Arthur. It seems that he was taken by magic and buried in the Isle of Avalon by Morgan le Fay. There he dwells in an underground palace and, when he wants an airing, he gets changed into a Raven. Therefore, no one would think of harming a Raven as it might be King Arthur. In general, their deep solemn voice made people think that there was something unearthly and ominous about them. Their presence on a battlefield was because of the slain warriors. Therefore, they represented a bird of death, gloom, doom and the night. Their flesh was forbidden to be eaten as they were carrion eaters. In some parts of Germany, these birds were believed to be the souls of the damned and that witches rode on their backs instead of brooms.

The Romans said that Raven broth was good for eyesight. There was a Czecko-Slovakian belief that he who ate three hearts of this bird reduced to ashes would become an unerring shot, the reason being that Ravens were said to eat the eyes out of carrion first. Even in death, his dried head and beak became a talisman and his other parts went into the witches' brew! Pliny tells of an amazing fact (?) that they conceive through their beaks and a woman who ate a Raven's egg gave birth through her mouth.

How about this one? In Greece, if you ate Raven's eggs, they would turn your gray hair to black but you had to oil your teeth or they would turn black too. These birds were also said to influence the weather. They brought rain to ancient Greece. The Chinese said that if a Raven/Crow alighted on your ship's mast, they should be thrown crumbs so that these birds would talk to the powers of the air and bring good winds.

In the Tower of London there have been Ravens for centuries. They were said to have made so much noise when the Normans attacked that the tower was saved. When it was bombed in World War II, all the Ravens left. This was a disaster as it was said that when Ravens left their home, it foretold the downfall of the owner of the property. Winston Churchill quickly changed this misfortune by importing young birds from Northern Wales and Southwest Scotland. Their wings were clipped and they were placed in the Tower. Great Britain was saved!

In this country there are many stories of how the Raven was once white but was turned black through his misdeeds. He was thought of as a trickster, transformer and creator to the tribes of the North Pacific coast and the people of British Columbia. While he gave them many gifts, he also made fools out of them. The Alaskan Tlingit worshipped a Raven God, as he survived the Flood and created man out of leaves, but he was a minor part in their religion. They thought that he gave all the birds their plumages and even went to Sitka to arrange for their habits and abodes! His good nature was seen in having given the Robin its lovely voice, the Hummingbird its beautiful colors, giving the Woodpeckers the stripes on their backs and tying up the Blue Jay's head feathers in a topknot. He was said to have released daylight, caused tides to ebb and flow, and planned the use of fire for the use of man. The Tlingit and the Haida said that their ancestors were present when the Raven opened up the daylight box and freed the sun, moon and stars. He also journeyed like Jonah in the body of a whale. He could turn himself into a man, animal or bird, or any combination of these. He is seen on totem poles with the sun, moon and stars. He can be identified by his wings, feet, straight bill and black color. Along with his good aspects, there was his greed and voraciousness. Once he was said to have lost his beak trying to eat the bait off a halibut hook. The fisherman took the object to the chief who could not figure out what it was. The crafty Raven turned himself into a man and covered his face with a blanket and told the chief he might be able to help. He took it in his hands and pretended to examine it. Then he clamped it back onto his face and flew away laughing at the men.

He was a hero-bird to the Cherokee who said that he became black by trying to bring fire out of a hollow tree that had been hit by lightning by the "Thunderer." Here is another story of how he became black. It seems that he was in a house with a Petrel and played a trick on the seabird. The Petrel got mad and the Raven tried to escape through the smoke hole but got stuck. The Petrel then made a fire under the hole and the smoke turned the Raven's feathers from white to black. See the Snowy Owl for a similar story.

Finally, the Zoroastrians said that he was good as he removed all the pollution-carrion from the earth. The Celtics had a phrase "Raven's knowledge" which meant knowing all about the living, the dead and seeing everything. Do not forget the lines of Edgar Allen Poe's poem: "Quote the Raven nevermore."

Raven, Black *Corvus umbrinus*

To some of the Sudanese of Upper Egypt, this bird was considered as their uncle and they extracted blood money from anyone who killed their relative. Any bird killed was given a solemn burial. The body was carried on a bier to the grave with flags and shouting "la il allah" just as if it had been a real relative.

Redpoll, Common *Carduelis flammea 5"*

Goldfinches and some of their allies have the generic name of "Carduelis" which is derived from the Latin "carduus" or thistle. Many species are fond of thistle seeds. Redpolls, who are a northern circumpolar bird, are gregarious and nest in colonies. They have a red cap and black chin and their song is a trilling twitter.

The Inuits tell of how long ago, when the endless night covered the world, there was no fire as it was guarded from people by a fierce bear in the north. At that time the little Redpoll was a brown bird. He heard of the complaint of no fire and the dread of the bear so he set out to steal it. After many adventures to solve this problem, he was able to steal a live ember in his beak and brought it back to the men. Its glow reflected onto its head and

183

breast and so, today, he wears the red color as an emblem and proof of the legend. The Inuit love this bird for that reason as well as for its cheery appearance and song.

Rhea

These big, easily tamed Ratites of South America, where they are called Ostriches, need close watching. They are 4-5 feet tall and can weigh fifty pounds. The big problem with them is their real love of eating gardens and house plants. To escape they really can run. They make a good zoo bird though.

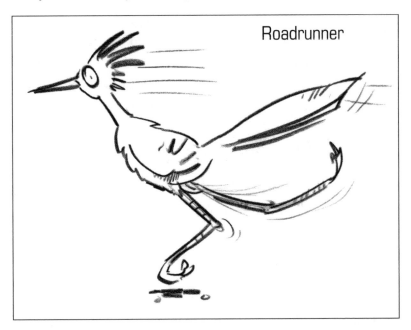

Roadrunner

Roadrunner *Geococcycx californianus 23"*

This odd looking bird of the Cuckoo family is called the "Chaparral cock" of the American Southwest deserts due to its habits. They are a streaked brown and white bird with two toes going forward and two backward. They are ground dwellers and have strong heavy bills and legs and a silly bushy crest. They are considered brave as they feed on snakes and lizards. These they kill by pounding them with their heavy bills and then swallowing them down head first. They have been clocked at fifteen miles an hour making the Pueblo say their running was like flying. To these people, they were the keeper of endurance and courage. Their footprints look like an X. As it points in no direction and leaves no path, war parties copied them. From this bird, they would take an upper tail feather and an under one and cross them like an X. Then they would put this in their moccasin between the middle and second toes to give them courage. They used these birds in scalp ceremonies and placed their feathers inside a pottery drum where they were also crossed. Along with these feathers were placed two pieces of crossed yucca to symbolize bravery. Added to this, the Roadrunner is the famous cartoon bird!

Robin, American *Turdus migratorius 10"*

These Thrushes can be found from Alaska and Canada down to Southern Mexico. These common lawn birds are a gray-brown above with darker heads and tails, brick red underparts and a white lower belly. The female is a paler version of the male. Members of this family are famous for their songs and are only absent from the Antarctic, the frigid North and some Polynesian Islands. In New Zealand, the European Blackbird and the European (English) Robin were introduced in 1862 to make the early settlers feel at home.

The name "Robin" has been used all over the world where English is spoken. The American Robin seems to be one of the leaders of the dawn chorus well before the sun rises. Maybe they inspired the saying "the early bird gets the worm" as they do love them! In the spring, when the returning Robins arrive in flocks on your lawn, you realize how true is the saying "birds of a feather flock together."

In folklore, this bird was the older brother of the Blue Jay and was constantly upbraiding him for his bad ways. The Tlingit said that the Raven gave him his voice so that he could give pleasure. The Chippewa said that he was so friendly because once his Father sent him on a long journey. This was too hard for the son so he was turned into a Robin so he could cheer people with his voice even though he never could become a warrior. The Iroquois planted cherry trees near their lodges "for the Robin." His name "Jis-go-ga" has been borne by many famous chiefs. The Robin is generally thought of as the harbinger of good fortune and good luck if it is not injured or chased away. Finding its nest was a good omen, but if you took away an egg, bad luck would follow you. To the Pueblo, the red of it breast represented the Southeast. The Neskapi Tribe of Labrador explained its red breast by a folktale. A woman was pushed into a fire by her angry husband and so returned to life as a Robin.

Robin, European *Erithacus rubecula 5 1/2"*

Thrushes get their name from the Anglo-Saxon word "thrysre." This little bird, often called the English Robin, is found in Europe, Asia Minor and Northern Africa. It can be found in Christian literature and legends, and symbolized confiding trust. In Sweden, they told of how the Virgin Mary got a fly in her eye. The Swallow deftly removed it with his flat tail and the Robin turned up with water in its beak to soothe it. At Christmas time they put out sheaves of wheat for this bird to eat.

European Robin

The people on the Isle of Guernsey said that this was the bird that brought them fire.

One of the most popular tales is of a small olive-brown bird who was at the stable in Bethlehem and was asleep. The angel choir awakened him and he noticed that the shepherd's fire was dying out. He fanned the embers which awakened the shepherds and his breast became red from the heat and has been that way ever since. He was also said to have tried to help Jesus on the Cross and absorbed his blood onto his breast. There are skeptics who say not at all. The color was due to the fact that the bird had a habit of taking a drop of water each day down to Hell to cool the tongues of the people there. The heat of the inferno scorched it red. Take your choice!

This is the bird of the nursery legends, the Cock Robin and the Robin Redbreast. These birds forage in leaves which may have been the origin of the stories that this bird covered corpses with leaves. Before Christmas cards in the eighteen sixties, Victorian writers used notepaper with a Robin on it and often carrying a letter in its beak. Postmen in those days were called "Robins" because of their red coats. When the color was changed to blue, the name got dropped. Today, there are red pillar mailboxes on corners in England and Robins are still on Christmas cards.

There are many stories about what happened to you if you kill one of these birds. In Ireland, your hand would swell. In Suffolk, a schoolboy's bad handwriting was because he had killed one, and others having done the same would get the shakes. In Bohemia, destroying a nest brought palsy to the hand of the destroyer, and in the Tyrol, it brought epilepsy. In Dartmoor, England, taking a Robin's nest would be followed by the smashing of your crockery. In Wales, stealing its eggs meant becoming a victim of witches or the devil. Finally, in Scotland, it was a sin to kill one as it "had a drop of God's blood in its veins."

They were said to be regular churchgoers. One lived in Canterbury Cathedral in the 17th century, and in 1880 one perched on the organ of Bristol Cathedral and sang. In 1695, at Westminster Abbey, one hopped about the hearse of Queen Mary II lying in state before her funeral!

Rook *Corvus frugilegus 18"*

These birds nest together in large numbers giving rise to the word "rookery." This word is applied to other kinds of species as well. You can find these birds near cultivated fields and woods all over Eurasia. Their plumage is sort of shaggy looking and glossy black. They have a long straight bill with a pale area around it.

In Kerry, Ireland, they said that these birds were bad land-lords as they stole vegetables from peasant gardens. If a rookery is deserted, then bad luck will befall the owner of the land. In earlier days, "to rook" was a verb meaning cheating and a "rookery" was a gambling den, brothel or barracks for hoboes!

Ruff *Philomachus pugnax male 12" female 9"*

The male of this species is called the Ruff while the female is the Reeve. At mating time, the Ruff grows an amazing frill of erect feathers around its neck - hence, the word. No two birds look alike being a combination of buff, chestnut, white, black and purple feathers. These birds can be found from Northern Europe to South Asia and North Africa. Occasionally, they turn up in North America. The males do an odd dance at mating time. This is when their ruffs are exposed and they stick their bills in the earth and quiver all over. This is done on a special dancing ground for males called a "lek." This is to attract the females. In 1769, they were considered a delicious market bird having been fattened up first on bread, milk and hempseed.

Sandpipers in general *5-11"*

The small ones are called "peeps" and look quite a lot alike with their brown-gray back feathers and lighter colors below. They are running beach birds always ahead of the incoming waves. Aristotle said that, in Egypt, they flew into the mouths of Crocodiles and picked out the flesh that had adhered to their teeth. "Caldidris" was a pure white bird very prized in Europe in the Middle Ages. One would be placed next to a dying person, and if the bird looked away, it was the truth. If not the bird would cure the patient by sucking up the disease and spitting it into the sky. For generations sandpipers were shot or taken in nets for food. They placed painted decoys that resembled the birds to lure them in. The opinion seemed to be that the Red Knot *Calidris canutus* was even better eating than the well-fed Ruff (see above).

Sandpiper, Spotted
Actitis macularia 7 1/2"

These birds are widespread on lakes, shores, rivers, streams and marshes all over the United States and winter into South America. This little spotted bird who is forever nodding and teetering on land is supposed to be a forecaster of rain. Rainmaking is applied to many Sandpipers. The word Sandpiper comes from the fact that they are birds of the shore and sand and make piping noises.

Screamers *28-33"*

These long-legged swimming birds look like small Turkeys. They are related to waterfowl but really do not resemble them. They have a horn on the forehead, two sharp spurs on the forward part of their wings and have elongated toes. The three species, who live in South America, have feathers that grow all over their bodies and not in the usual feather tracts. They get their name from their cry and so are often called "Chaja" for that reason. They annoy the South American hunters as they fly to tree tops when disturbed. There they can view what is going on and alarm all the game in the area. They are a common zoo bird!

Secretary Bird

Secretary Bird *Sagittarius serpentarius 46"*

This long-legged Hawk (in its own family) was known as Sagittarius or Archer from its striding gait which was likened to a bowman advancing to shoot. Somehow, the name got corrupted to secretarius. They are gray, white and black and are found south of the Sahara. They hunt on foot in a zigzag fashion looking for snakes, small mammals, large insects, young birds and eggs. They are famous snake-killers. They have a pair of elongated feathers on the back of the nape and head that hang loosely like a bunch of quills. These can be erected and dilated in excitement. Actually, the name Secretary Bird comes from the old-fashioned clerk whose quill was supposed to be put above the ear!

Shearwaters in general

These drab colored tube-nosed birds of 15 to 25 inches have long pointed wings and roam over the oceans of the world. Their name came from fishermen who noticed that these birds swung back and forth, to and fro, and seem to shear the water. In Australia and New Zealand, they are called "Mutton Birds." They were used by the early settlers for food. Even today, they are used for food and there is a thriving, regulated industry on their breeding grounds. The young are taken from the nest after fledging and having been deserted by their parents. They are quickly killed, hung up to drain their precious stomach oil and then are processed for canning. They are sold as "Tasmanian Squabs." They are not fishy and make very good eating.

Shearwater, Manx *Puffinus puffinus 14"*

These birds cover both sides of the North Atlantic and the Mediterranean where they stay in groups rather than following ships. They do not breed on the Isle of Man for which they were named. The French, Moslem and Turks said that these birds never rested and that their somber plumage meant that they were the souls of the condemned but they were also weather prophets!

One of these birds was taken from its nest on Skohlolm Island, Wales, to the Boston airport in a crate. There it was liberated and the bird was back in its nest twelve days and thirteen hours later. This was not its usual migratory route but it must have averaged two hundred and fifty miles a day. Thirty-two hundred miles must have been its shortest route. How is that for homing!

Shrike, Loggerhead *Lanius ludovicianus 9"*

They have another name and that is "Butcher-bird." The Latin word "Lanius" means butcher. These big headed birds are found from Southern Canada to Southern Mexico. There are two species of Shrikes in North America and the rest of this large family are worldwide. They have a gray-blue head and back, are white below and have a black facial mask.

A 1836 book tells of how these birds baited thorns with grasshoppers to decoy the smaller insect-eating birds into situations where they could be easily seized! They were said to believe in a well stocked larder and would not eat until they had a goodly supply. They were sometimes called the "Nine-killers" in America for their supposed preference for collecting that number of prey. They actually do impale mice and small birds on thorns

193

or sharp places. They are a perching bird with no talons with which to rip open their food. Instead, they have a broad, stout, very sharp bill that is notched at the tip. Added to this, they have on each side of the upper bill a tomial tooth which aids them in killing their prey.

The Pueblo called them "Messenger-birds" with their strident voices. They also called them "a brilliant bird but an evil one" so were reluctant to use them in ceremonies.

Siskin *Carduelis spinus 4 1/2"*

These are a streaked greenish bird with a pointed bill and have a patch of yellow on the wings and tail. This common little bird is found all over the Northern Hemisphere. You see them most often when, after the breeding season, they gather in flocks often with Goldfinches. What makes them interesting is that, in the Tyrol and in Bohemia, they were said to possess a magic stone (like the Swallow) and the owner of such could make himself invisible!

Skimmer, Black *Rynchops niger 18"*

These are the only birds who have the lower bill longer than the upper. This bill is bright red and black-tipped. This adaptation acts like a knife blade as the birds skim along the water looking for food. It also gives rise to their other name of "Cut-water-bird." The bills of the young are the same length until they are half grown. These birds are black-headed, black-backed with white underparts and red feet and legs. These odd, long-winged birds can be found, usually in flocks, from Long Island Sound to both sides of South America.

Skua/Jaeger *Sterocorarius 19-23"*

There are three species in the Gull family that we call Jaegers and two that are called Skuas. In Europe, they are all called Skuas. Skua is an old Norwegian name and comes from the Dutch and German. From the Norse, we get "jaga" meaning to hunt and so are called Jaegers and Skuas from their habits and cries. They are dark pelagic seabirds with strong wings and a powerful flight. They can be told by their elongated central tail feathers. The three Jaegers nest in the Arctic and then go further south in the Atlantic and Pacific. The Great Skua breeds in Northern Europe and Iceland and winters in the North Atlantic. The South Polar Skua nests in Antarctica and winters (our summers) in the North Atlantic and Pacific. These aggressive birds make smaller birds disgorge their already swallowed prey which they have caught. They are extremely fond of other birds' eggs and young, lemmings and small rodents. From their habits they get the name of "Teasers or Boatswains." In the Shetlands, a fine was levied for killing one as it was believed that they protected their sheep from Eagles.

Skylark *Alauda arvensis (probably) 7"*

This is one of the most celebrated birds in literature. They are found from Europe to Africa to India. Some were successfully introduced into Hawaii and New Zealand. It was the "Blithe Spirit" of Percy Bysshe Shelley's poem "To a Skylark." They also inspired Tennyson and Wordsworth with their renowned singing which they do as they fly. The courting flight of the male is spectacular. In the Scottish Highlands, to learn what it was singing, you just lay down and listened. In rural Great Britain, to improve your voice you drank three Lark eggs. In the second century, you ate a Lark to cure colic. While this bird is said to be of spiritual inspiration, they were likewise good in pies and they were sold in markets. For example in the winter of 1867-68, the Town of Dieppe sent 1,255,500 Larks valued at 2260 pounds to the London markets.

Snipe, Common *Gallinago gallinago 11"*

The word Snipe comes from the Anglo-Saxon word "snite" as well as from the use of its bill and the noise it makes with its wings. They are circumpolar in the Northern Hemisphere and they winter below the Equator. This bird is very fast on the wing and hard to shoot because of its erratic flight. In its mating flight, it makes a loud noise caused by air rushing through its wings and tail feathers as it drops to the ground. As a result, the people of Northern Europe thought that this bird must have the power to make real thunder. It became a storm spirit as its drumming at mating time resembled the roar of the wind and its zigzag flight was like lightning. They are a stocky, short-legged, short-necked and long-billed bird of the woodlands and swamps. They are boldly patterned above, white below with a distinctive striped head and rusty tail.

In the United States, they used to be known as Wilson's Snipe. The Pueblo said that it was the pet of the clouds as his footprint decorated the Horned Water Snake who controlled the underground waterways. These secretive birds use their long bill for probing in the mud of marshes, swamps and meadows looking for food. Because of their habits and habitats, they were known as "Gutter-snipes." Now the term is an insulting word for a rundown bum. "Sniping" was a military term for a sharpshooter hitting every target. A "snipe-hunt" is simply a joke to fool an unsuspecting person!

Sparrow, Chipping
Spizella passerina 5 1/2"

This is a common bird of the lawns and gardens with a reddish cap, white breast and two white wing bars. They have a black line through the eyes with a white one over it. Their song is a trill of chirps all on one note. They range from Canada to Nicaragua. This little bird likes to use hair in its compact nest. Horse-hair is getting scarce so ladies are said to beware as headaches and baldness could come their way!

Sparrow, House *Passer domesticus 6"*

Sparrow comes from the Indo-European word "spe'r" and was a general term for a small bird. The male of this species has a black throat, white cheeks and a chestnut nape while his mate is a dull brown. In the cities they are very sooty looking and dull colored from their surroundings. In Egyptian hieroglyphics they stood for enemy, connoted bad luck and were a symbol of lasciviousness. Keeping one in a cage was bad luck unless it was an albino. If you ate one in the Tyrol, you would get St. Vitus Dance. However, in many places, vendors used to pluck them, dip them in a spicy sauce, place several on a stick and brown them over a fire to make a meal for a hungry person. They were said to be sacred to Venus and lustful as the devil took their form.

There was a Russian story of how when Jesus was on the Cross, these Sparrows kept chirping "jif, jif" meaning he was living, so he could be further tormented. At the same time, the

Swallows were calling "ummer, ummer" meaning dead. As a result, the Swallows have been blessed and the Sparrows cursed. Their legs are tied with an invisible bond so all they can do is hop! They were used as rent money in England during the 15th and 16th centuries. They were the commonest species in England and lived near farms and houses hence the name House Sparrow. When they were introduced into the United States, they acquired the name of English Sparrow. They are known all over the world as a robber of grain and have thrived on man's labor.

Today, many Turkeys are raised over wire because they are susceptible to a disease of the intestines known as "blackhead." It is a protozoan type that passes one of its cycles in damp ground. It is carried and spread by this Sparrow who is immune to it but can bring it into barnyards and infect the Turkeys.

Here is a quaint Victorian tale. A wicked boy went to rob a Sparrow's nest and was moved to shame to find it lined with the Issac Watt hymn "Oh, God our help in ages past." When the boy became a man, he was turned into a Sparrow and was solicited in Piccadilly by ladies turned "Sparrow Catchers." These birds were tethered and used as toys to amuse children and called Philip Sparrow. They were also said to have killed "Cock Robin!"

Sparrow, White-throated
Zonotrichia albicollis 6 3/4"

This well named bird, with its white throat and black and white head stripes, lives from Canada to Mexico. They breed in the northern sections and winter further south. The song of this bird will tell you where you are. If in New England, then it will sing "Old Sam Peabody, Peabody, Peabody." Should you be in Canada, it will sing "Sweet Canada, Canada, Canada."

Spoonbill

Spoonbill *Platalea leucorodia 34"*

This basically white bird with a spoonlike bill is uncommon and scattered in it distribution. In the breeding season the adults grow a long crest. The young have black-tipped wings that they lose on maturity. The European food report of 1542 said that these birds were "lighter of digestion" than a Bittern but not quite as good as Heron. However, their young were equal to the young of Herons.

Spoonbill, Roseate *Platela ajaja 32"*

In the southern United States, these flaming pink to red birds are called "Pink Curlews." They have greenish unfeathered heads and black tips to their primary feathers that are seen only in flight. Unlike Herons and Egrets, who visually look for their prey, these birds hunt by touch. They swing their heads to and fro while pacing the shallows for prey. When they find a school of small fish, they dart about frantically and spread one or both wings. They become "beaters" for other birds like the Cormorant who come in to feed on the confused fish. These birds fly with their necks outstretched and often glide.

Beginning in 1850, they almost became extinct along with the Herons and Egrets as they were slaughtered for their plumes. Spoonbills were not as popular as the others since their colors fade fast but their wings made great fans. In 1910, the Audubon plume bill was passed and crippled the feather industry but it was almost too late for this bird. They have made a slow comeback but are still rare and a thrilling sight to behold. Their bills really do look like a spoon!

Starling, Common *Sturnus vulgaris 8 1/2"*

This word comes from the Old English "Stern" and from its fall plumage that resembles little stars. This European bird was once a bird of good luck but it multiplied so fast that it became a nuisance and now is a token of evil. These birds were said to take hair combings from women and put them in their nests. Superstition had it that the owner of the hair was endangered as she was involved in the bird's evil actions.

Pliny alluded to the fact that they could be trained to amuse the young Caesars and utter Greek and Latin words. In the 17th and 18th centuries, they caused great losses to the crops used in the thatching of roofs. Their numbers were so great that they bent over the reeds, snapping them so that they could not develop. Also, their guano soiled the reeds so that they could not be sold. There is a record of their damaging one hundred pounds of reeds in one night.

Unfortunately for the United States, a Eugene Schieffelin liberated eighty Starling in Central Park New York, on March 6, 1890. They were part of his sentimental plan to release every species of birds known in Shakespeare's plays into that park. Within ten years they had reached New Haven and in ten more had multiplied enough to reach the Middle West and now are found all over North America. South America and the frigid areas have yet to host them. These flocks are a real pest and a plague to cities because of their numbers and excrements. They take over nesting areas of other birds such as Bluebirds and Woodpeckers and seem to nest anywhere. They can be seen in whirling flocks too big to count and are a real menace to aircraft. They are a good example of the dangers of introducing foreign birds and animals where they are not native and can create population explosions. Man has helped this bird cover most of the world. This "blackbird" (not a true one) can be identified in flight by its short tail that makes it look like a triangle with one end slightly squared off. Real Blackbirds have longer tails.

Stork, White *Ciconia ciconia 40"*

Pictures of Herons, Cranes or Storks were found in the Caves of Lascaux, France, dating from the Old Stone Age. Aristotle wrote in 330 B.C. that it was a crime to kill one as it protected homes from evil and lightning. The Romans agreed and passed a law called "Lex Ciconia," or Stork Law, requiring children to care for needy parents when they became elderly. Throughout Europe, they were known as the symbol of filial piety, faithfulness, home life and marriage. These black and white birds return each year to the same chimney. They were said to bring babies and bite the mother's foot so she had to stay in bed and care for the newborn. In Germany, they said that one on the roof or flying by meant a birth. These Storks were said to pick up babies from the marshes, wells, springs, ponds and stones where the souls of the unborn resided. Hans Christian Andersen immortalized the myth of dropping the baby down the chimney! These birds were said to be guardians of the house and would not allow free love. The offenders were pecked to death by their long spear-like bills!

When they returned in the spring, you could tell what sort of a summer was ahead. If the birds were clean and white, then all would be well and there would be heat and sunshine. However, if they were dirty then a bad one was ahead. In Sweden, they said that they lost their voices when flying around the Cross saying "styrka, styrka" meaning strengthen ye, strengthen ye. A close sounding word to Stork. There was another belief that if a Stork left its nest, disaster would follow. At the siege of Aquleia in 451 B.C. the Romans held out bravely against Attila the Hun. Smartly, he noticed that the Storks were leaving their nest with their young. He realized that the city would give up and so attacked again and proved the Storks were correct!

You can find these big birds from Europe to Asia, China and Japan. For generations great flocks leave in the fall and return in the spring again. For centuries people wondered where these birds went. Did they go to the moon or hibernate in swamps and ponds? Slowly, people began to realize that migration might occur. They had the answer. The larger, broad-winged ones like the Stork, would carry the smaller ones as live freight on their backs both spring and fall. Maybe they went to some place like Africa? Correct.

Leonardo da Vinci said that a Stork could cure himself of any illness by drinking salt water. They could kill serpents and their stomachs were used as a specific for the murrain of sheep and goats. Young birds, when eaten, were a good prophylactic against ophthalmia. Lastly, like the Heron, they foretold rain by flying low, and they waxed and waned with the moon. They were plump when the moon was full and lean when it was waning!

Stork, Wood *Mycteria americana 47"*

The Old English word "storc" later became Stork. The Wood Stork is found in Central and South America and in the United States mainly in Florida. They are moving slowly northward. They nest in big colonies with big nests. Their food depends on the water levels so their numbers fluctuate from year to year. They are known as "Wood Ibis and Flatheads" because of their bare heads and horny crown plate. They get called "Preacher" because of their black and white plumage and somber appearance. Their flight feathers and tails are black in contrast to the white of their bodies.

The Aztec said if any one stole a Wood Stork, the city in which they lived would come to grief. The Arawak loved this bird and the Hummingbird as the two of them stole the original tobacco seed and brought it to them.

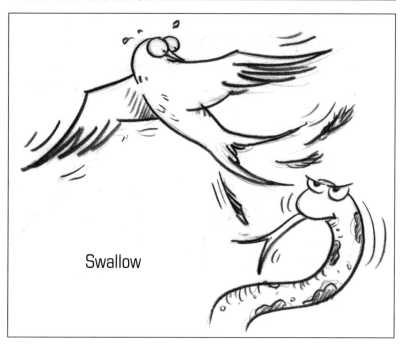

Swallow

Swallow/Martin in general *4-9"*

All over the world, these birds mean spring and sunshine with their name coming from the Anglo-Saxon "svalewe" and the Old Norse "svalva." Martin is a newer word and used in heraldry. The two names are used interchangeably, Swallow being the most popular. In Scandinavia, one of these birds was said to have hovered near the Cross and cried, "svalva, svalva" meaning console, console hence the name "svalow." They were the birds of consolation and used in art as a symbol of the Resurrection. These friendly, insect-eating birds appear in the spring and leave in the fall. This habit likened them to rebirth and are frequently seen in Nativity paintings nesting in the eaves.

There are several tales of how the Swallow got its forked tail. The most common one is from flying up to the sun to bring back fire and a spark burned a hole in its tail. My favorite one is about the Garden of Eden. There were Swallows flying around and trying to stop the machinations of Adam and Eve. The serpent was not happy about these Swallows so took a swipe at the birds but he missed and only got the center tail feathers!

The Romans liked them and felt that it was lucky to have one around your house. They were sacred to the household gods so it was unlucky to harm one. The Romans took mother Swallows off their nests and tied silk colored threads to their legs when they went to the chariot races. Then they would liberate the birds who headed back to their nests with the victory news. The Greeks liked them to nest in their homes as a good omen and, as they were divine, they were allowed to nest in the Temples of Athens and Olympia. Before that though, if a Greek woman found one in her house, she would pour oil on it to remove any bad luck. She then liberated the poor soaked bird who must have had a bad time flying!

The Koran said that they were sacred to Islam and saved Mecca from the Abysinnian (Christian) army in the year of Mohammed's birth. It was said that God gave each bird three stones for his bill and two for his feet. The Swallows dropped these on the men and elephants killing them. One man escaped and fled to tell his king but the birds followed and killed him too. History tells of how these stones were filled with a small pox, the pustules of which were called by an Arabic name meaning small stones.

There are many stories of how these birds own two stones. The red one cured invalids and the black one brought good fortune. A Swallow found on the seashore had a stone that could restore sight as Longfellow referred to in his poem "Evangeline." Ancient authors said that these birds are blind at birth (like most perching birds). The parents would go searching for the plant called

Chelidonium or Swallow herb to give the babies sight. An old book on falconry said that if a Hawk's eye gets injured, put the juice of celodine in the eye and it would be cured. If it happened to occur after the growing season, you took the dried powder of the plant and blew it with a quill into the eye and it would be cured. Any stone that you could find in a Swallow's nest would cure eye problems. Alas, there are no such stones!

These birds were poorly judged in the early days as they were said to hibernate all winter in the mud of ponds or else go to the moon. However, when they returned in the spring, you could put away your winter clothes, and if in Scotland plant your peas. In the Carpathian Mountains if you had freckles, you could transfer them to the first Swallow you saw in spring by uttering certain commands. In Norfolk, England, people thought that the gathering of these birds around a church in the fall meant they were deciding who would die before they returned! It was bad luck to steal an egg of this bird as rain would then destroy your crop and your cows would cease giving milk. Boiled Swallows were a remedy for a bite from a mad dog. The heart of this bird worn around your neck could make you more attractive and strengthen your memory. They were said to be lucky on land but not if seen at sea. Cleopatra once saw one on the masthead of her ship and abandoned her voyage! They are among the earliest fall migrants and can be seen by the hundreds sitting on telegraph poles waiting to take off on their southward trek. In heraldry, the Martin/Swallow was the cadence for the fourth son. The first inherited, the second became a soldier, the third entered the church and the fourth flew away to seek his fortune as there was nothing left for him. This was supposed to signify that as these birds seldom light on land so younger brothers have little land on which to rest. They do have the wings of their endeavors, so like Swallows become travelers! While one Swallow does not make a summer, it does mean that it is coming. Peking, China, was once known as the Swallow City.

Swallow, Barn _Hirundo rustica 7"_

These birds are truly swallow-tailed. They are blue above and reddish below and are widespread in the Northern Hemisphere. You will have good luck if these birds nest in your barn or eaves and will help keep down the insect population. Do not destroy a nest or bad luck will come your way.

Swallow, Cliff _Petrochelidon pyrrhonota 6"_

From Alaska and Canada to Mexico, you can see these square-tailed rusty, rumped birds. Note the scientific name which refers to the Swallow herb! These are the famous birds of the California Mission of San Juan Capistrano. It is said that since the Spanish colonial times, these birds have arrived back on St. Joseph's Day which is March 19th. They are said to leave for the south on St. John's Day, October 23rd. There are usually a few birds around on these days to keep the story alive. They do not all arrive or leave on these days.

Swallow, Violet-green
Tachycincta thalassina 5 1/2"

These colorful birds of Western Canada down to Mexico have a purple-green glossy back, white breast and a white patch that almost meets over the tail. These birds were said to have been very kind when they gave some of their pretty feathers to the originally dull-colored Hummingbirds to make them beautiful. Native American rain priests used their feathers, along with the Cliff Swallow's and those of the Rough-winged Swallows *Stelgidopteryx ruficollis*. In order to catch these birds for their ceremonies, they had to stretch nets of horsehair across streams and ponds.

Swan, Black *Cygnus atratus 55"*

This beautiful black bird with curly feathers on its backend has a bright red bill and white wing tips that can be seen only in flight. It is native to Australia and Tasmania and appears on the armorial standard of Western Australia and some stamps. The Dutch discovered this bird in 1697 and took it to Batavia and then to Europe. It domesticates easily and is raised successfully in captivity. Some of the stock has been taken to New Zealand, where it has become semi-wild and has adjusted to the climate. Today, you can see them in most parks and zoos.

Swan, Mute *Cygnus olor 60"*

This graceful, large bird is not mute. It can be identified by the knob on its bill. They were originally from Northern Europe where they were domesticated first for food and then for their beauty. Now they are all over temperate Eurasia and have been domesticated in the United States and Australia and many, many have gone wild. The word Swan is an Old English name. Swans were domesticated prior to the 12th century. The male is the cob, the female is the pen and the young are called cygnets.

They have a unique position in England as the Birds of the Crown. An early king proclaimed that they were all his and, for a fee, a few privileged people could keep their own herd. In 1500, nine hundred marks were registered with the Royal Swan Keeper. These marks were mainly on the upper bill but some were on the lower one, legs, feet or wings in various combinations. The royal one was two lengthwise and three across. There were severe fines for infringing on Swan-rights and a registry was kept of the marks and the owners. The official was called "Master of the King's or Queen's Game of Swans" and shortened to "Chief Swanherd or Swannerd." He had deputies to cover England, their main duty being the maintenance of the Swans of the Crown and seeing that the others were protected.

They were used as a holiday bird before the advent of the Turkey. Henry III had one hundred and twenty-five of them at a banquet in York for Christmas in 1251. Edward I, at his investiture as a knight, had swans decorated in gold net so that he could swear his oath to heaven on them. These birds along with the Peacock and the Pheasant were picked by knights to honor God, the Virgin or their lady love. In 1440, Frederick of Brandenberg started the Order of the Swan. It was the bird of Anne of Cleves, the Vintner's Company and Eton College and was used in heraldry until the Middle Ages. "Swan-upping" is the annual rounding up of the young birds in the late summer so they can be marked. There is a famous annual festival of this on the Thames River in England.

They can be seen in tapestries to show good luck and in Egyptian hieroglyphics stood for music. The Greeks claimed that Apollo was the God of Music who went across the sky each day in his swan drawn chariot. However, they are not great singers! Zeus was said to have used swan feathers to woo Leda. The story of Leda and the Swan is found throughout literature. These birds are superstitiously protected in Ireland because of the legend of Fionnula, the daughter of Lir, who was turned into a Swan and condemned to wander the lakes and ponds until Christianity was introduced. In County Mayo in Ireland, they said virgins got turned into Swans at their deaths. The Vikings recognized their migration habits and, in the 8th and 9th centuries, they followed their paths south when on raiding parties. In Northern lands, they said that lute players invited Swans to play in their concerts. In Iceland, they were supposed to sing like a violin in the long dark night of winter.

The expressions "I swan" or "it swans to me" meant a foreboding. The stories of Swan-maidens and Swan-shifts are found all over the world. The stories basically were that a group of Swans would fly over a nice lake and take off their "Swan-shifts" and bathe as Swan-maidens. Then along came men who stole their feathers and made the maidens their wives. However, before too long the wife would find her "Swan-shift," put it on and fly away. "Swan-songs" are known as anything representing the last work or performance of a musician or writer. In fables, it comes from the fact that Swans are supposed to sing a sweet "Swan-song" as they die. Alexander the Midian, in the first century, did a lot of field work on dying Swans and never heard one sing sweetly. Lohengrin, the Swan Knight of Richard Wagner's opera, appears and disappears in a Swan-drawn boat. Sailors love these birds as they mean good luck for the reason that they do not go all the way under water and the sailors do not want to either!

Swan, Trumpeter *Cygnus buccinator 60"*

Most Swans nest in the Northern Hemispheres and wander southward later. This bird is found on the western side of this country and in a few reserves. They can be told by the black facial skin that goes from the beak to the eyes making a V so the face appears black. They have a straight bill and sometimes a yellow spot in front of the eye. Their call is a loud bugle-like single or double honk.

In the 17th century, the Native Americans used its feathers in Headdresses. In 1789, the Hudson Bay Company began to hunt these birds when they were flightless in the summer. This is when they lose their wing feathers for almost a month while the new ones grow in. The Company sent these birds to England and really made a killing — both meanings. In the 19th century, their feathers were used for powder puffs and robes and their quill feathers for pens. John James Audubon even used them. Their skins were sold in New Orleans and their eggs went for four dollars apiece according to a 1892 catalog. They became extremely rare due to hunting and the loss of their breeding grounds to agriculture. They have been reintroduced to their former breeding areas and have made a fair comeback.

Swan, Tundra *Cygnus columbianus 52"*

This is our native Swan and was formerly known as the Whistling Swan. The Eurasian form of this bird is **Bewick's Swan** *Cygnus bewickii*. The Tundra Swan nests from Alaska to James Bay and comes south to both U.S. coasts in the winter. It now seems that "the song of the dying Swan" may not be a myth after all. In 1898 Daniel G. Elliot, an expert on Waterfowl, said that he shot one and as it fell, it uttered a song that he had never before heard. The waterfowl expert, the late H. Albert Hockbaum, writes of the departure song of this bird as "a melodious, soft, muted series of notes which in my experience always precedes the take-off run when the birds are about to fly. This pre-flight melody is probably the "swan-song" of legend, for when a swan is shot and falls crippled into the water, it utters this call as it tries in vain to join its fellows in the sky."

Swan, Whooper *Cygnus cygnus 60"*

This bird is often confused in stories with the Mute Swan. They are a Eurasian species closely related to the Trumpeter Swan. Their yellow bill can be seen as a straight line to the forehead and they hold their necks straight. They are the noisiest of the Swans and their double bugle-like call can be heard for great distances.

Swifts in general *4-9"*

Their speedy flight gave them their name. Some have been checked out at 100 miles an hour. They live on insects that they catch on the wing. They are basically grays and browns with short stiff tails and short legs. They collect small twigs in flight and glue them together with their saliva to make a nest on an inside wall.

In European tales, they are all mixed up with the Swallows even though they are not related. They both were said to hibernate all winter. They were said to carry bedbugs into houses but actually it would be hard to do as they nest in unused chimneys, otherwise the smoke and heat would cook them! In this country it was said that when the Cliff Swallows leave the San Juan Capistrano Mission in California, these birds spend the winter in their old nests!

Swift, Chimney *Chaetura pelagica 5 1/2"*

These summer residents of Eastern United States look like "flying cigars." They can be observed in large numbers at dusk when they descend into chimneys. For years no one knew where these birds spent the winter until in the Amazon River area some natives netted and roasted some. Many of these birds had bands on their legs and these got stuck in the teeth of the natives. This was a mystery so they took the bands to a local missionary who read the writing on the bands and sent them to the Fish and Wildlife Service in Washington D.C. The report came back that they had been banded on the roof area of the Yale-New Haven Hospital in Connecticut. The mystery of their wintering grounds had been revealed!

Swiftlet, Edible-nest and Gray-rumped Swiftlet
Collocalia inexpectata and Collocalia francica 4 1/2"

These birds of Malaysia and Indo-China make nests of pure saliva. They are top grade nests for commerce as well as a gastronomic treat. It has become a several thousand dollar industry. Native gatherers use bamboo ladders and long poles to knock off the nests from the cave ceilings and walls as soon as they are built. These birds make a second nest that is almost as pure and then if needed a third one that has impurities in it. The first nests are sold as they are and command the highest prices. The next two are pressed to remove the impurities and the protein rich gelatin that is left is made into chips called "Dragon's Teeth." Some nests are made into soup with medicinal properties that when combined with ginseng are capable of restoring life to an almost dead person!

Tanagers mostly under 8"

This name comes from the Tupi Indians of the Amazon who called them "tangara" and the quasi-Latin "tanagra." Finally, in the 19th century they became Tanagers. The 222 species of these birds live in the tropical or subtropical areas of the Americas. They have stout notched bills and in some cases both the males and the females are very brightly colored.

The Pawnee have a story of the Creation involving these birds. At one point in folklore, all the people were transferred into a bird or an animal but they had a choice. A young man said to his wife and sister "come with me to the timber, where we will stay. My father is the Sun, and so we will be red." As soon as he had said that, they were turned into red birds. The man was very red with two black streaks down from his eyes and the women were browner with back streaks. They flew to the timber and that is where they can be found.

Tanager, Brazilian
Rhamphocelus bresilius 9"

Here again the male is colorful and the female is dull and they look a lot like the **Scarlet Tanagers** *Piranga olivacae* but they live all year in South America. This bird has the distinction of probably being one of the first birds ever described. This was in 1555 by Belonius.

Tanager, Hepatic *Piranga flava 8"*

The four *Piranga* Tanagers have brightly colored males with red on them and olive colored females. They all migrate into the United States for the summer from South America. This bird visits the Southwest where the male is reddish with gray cheek patches and flanks. The Native Americans thought that this bird represented the zenith because of its dull red color.

Tanager, Scarlet *Piranga olivacea 7"*

One of the most resplendent Northeastern American birds with the males bright red body and black wings and tail. A sight to be seen, but in the fall he can be a mixture of red, yellow and black and not featured in bird books. The Winnebago used this bird in their witchcraft which was said to be a very profitable pastime!

Tanager, Summer *Piranga rubra 7 3/4"*

These birds are southern in range with the male being a rosy red all over. According to some Native American tribes, these birds were supposed to store up "a vast magazine of maize" to keep them going during the winter.

Tanager, Western
Piranga ludoviciana 7 1/4"

The male is a colorful bird with a red head, yellow wing bars and breast and a black back. In winter his head gets yellow. They are a western species and usually winter Mexico southward but occasionally will be found as far north as Oregon. Like the other Tanagers, they are insect-eating. To the Native Americans, this bird represented the north because of so much yellow in his plumage.

Tern, Arctic *Sterna paradisaea 15"*

Terns are streamlined white birds with forked tails and black caps. They are birds of the water who do not sit on it but dive into it for food. They fish with their bills turned down, a good clue as to their identity. This bird is famous for its pole to pole migrations. They do the circumpolar migration so that they see the sun twenty-four hours a day for eight months. In the other four, there is more daylight than darkness. Their summer and winter homes are about eleven thousand miles apart. By banding, one bird was known to have been twenty-seven years old. A chick banded in Labrador on July 23, 1928 was taken in Natal, Africa, on November 14, 1928. This was a nine thousand mile trek for a three and a half month old bird!

Tern, Common *Sterna hirundo 15"*

Terns get their name from the Norwegian "taerne" and the Dutch "sterna." They have another common name of "Sea Swallow" as their tails are elongated like a Swallow. They are also called "Mackerel Terns" as they follow schools of fish. In Ireland, they are the harbinger of a good fishing season. This bird and the Arctic Tern can easily be confused as they really do look alike. This bird's life history has been well documented and they return to the same place each year to nest. They do not go as far north as do the Arctic variety.

Tern, Sooty *Sterna fuscata 16"*

These strongly colored birds with black above and white below with a white forehead, reside on many tropical and

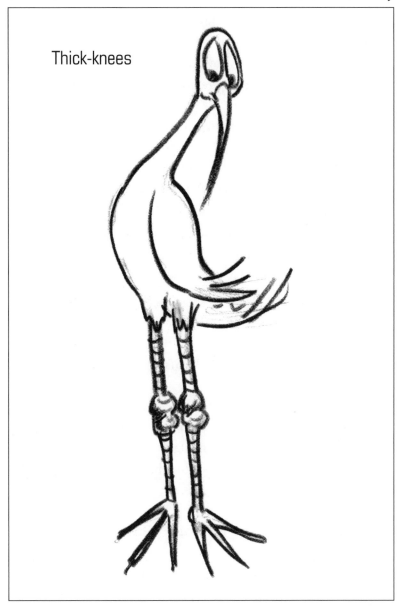

Thick-knees

oceanic islands. On Ascension Island just south of the Equator, in the South Atlantic, they nest every ten months. There is a big colony of them on the Dry Tortugas off Florida. There they nest

but once a year and lay one egg. There was a period when their eggs were taken and sold by the gallon to wholesale bakers. Luckily, these islands are now a National Monument so that these "Wideawakes" as they are often called have been saved.

Thick-knees *Burhinus 16"*

These birds may look like Bustards but are anatomically like shorebirds. They are found in Europe, North Africa and Southwest Asia. Like many running birds they have no hind toe. They are sometimes called "Stone Curlews" because they frequent pebbly, rough and dry areas. Their name comes from their very noticeable swollen heels or "knee" joints. They have long legs, plaintive cries and are most active at night. Because of this, the Egyptians associated these birds with the soul.

Thrasher, Brown *Toxostoma rufum 12"*

These birds are found in the East and Central United States in the summer. They are brownish above, have a long tail and a streaked breast. Often people mistake them for Thrushes. Old time Pennsylvania farmers associated their first song in spring as the time to plant the corn.

Thrushes in general *4 1/2 - 12"*

Thrushes are found in the Old and New Worlds but not in the frigid areas and some Pacific Islands. They are a large family of three hundred and six species and boast of the best singers. The tarsi of their legs are unscaled and called booted. They eat insects but not on the wing, like Flycatchers and others, and will eat fruit.

The Tsimishian people said that the California Condor made so much wind with his wings that it destroyed all the birds around so that he could get the wife of the Woodpecker who was a Thrush! Thrushes were supposed to be deaf and cast off their old legs every ten years and acquire new ones. In Europe, they were kept in cages for their lovely songs while the Romans fed them figs to fatten them up to eat.

Thrush family - Blackbird _Turdus_

In a district of the Sudan, it was forbidden to touch or remove the young of Blackbirds because the parents would avenge the wrong by causing stormy winds to blow and ruin the harvest. Wonder how they did it?

Thrush family - Blackbird
Turdus merula 10"

This all black Robin has an orange-yellow bill and an eye-ring. They are commonly found in parks, lawns and gardens of Europe. They were successfully introduced into New Zealand in 1862 along with the **Song Thrush** _Turdus philomelos_. This was to remind the early settlers of their homeland.

When St. Kevin was at the Rock in Glendalough, standing in prayer with his hands outstretched, a Blackbird laid an egg in them. The good saint was said to have remained motionless until it hatched. In India, they claimed that Buddha had one lay an egg on his bald head. He just went into a trance until it had hatched!

The nursery rhyme "sing a song of sixpence, a pocket full of rye, four and twenty blackbirds baked in a pie" was based on the fact that in the 16th century, Blackbirds were kept hidden in pies to amuse guests. Albino ones were never sold for food but kept as pets in aviaries. One more white to black bird story. Once upon a time these white birds became cold one day and sought refuge in a chimney. When they came out, they were black from the soot and have been that way ever since.

Thrush, Wood *Hylocichla mustelina 8"*

This pretty woodland Thrush is a plump bird that is brown above with a rusty head and lots of spots on its breast. They can be found from the Northeastern U.S. to Central America. The great naturalist Buffon really goofed when he said that American birds could not be melodious. He said that this bird represented the Song Thrush *Turdus philomelos* which somehow got around the northern seas and made its way to America. (They are both spotted on the breast). There, owing to a change in food and climate, its song became very harsh and unpleasant. He described it "as are all the cries of all the birds that live in wild countries inhabited by savages." This bird has probably the most beautiful and liquid song!

Thunderbird

This imaginary bird was the symbol of thunder and lightning. The Inuit, Native Americans, Caribs of Brazil, Cook Islanders off Australia, Beuchan and Batsu of Africa - to mention just a few - and many others all believed in this legendary bird. He was the source of lightning, thunder and sometimes beneficial rain. He was the Chief God and could be seen in the lightning which was either the flash of his eyes or his tracks across the sky. He was heard as thunder which could be the flapping of his wings or his voice.

Some people even thought that he carried a lake on his back when a downpour occurred. One of the earliest musical instruments once used by natives was a dry gourd filled with pebbles and decked with feathers and arrows which was rattled to imitate storms.

The Dakota pointed to his footprints twenty-five miles apart at Thunder Tracks near the source of the St. Peter's River. The Iroquois found him to be an invisible spirit called "Hino the Thunderer." The Nookta of Vancouver Island spoke of him as "Toofooch," the single survivor of four birds that fed on whales. The God Quawteaht took on the guise of a whale and lured three of them to strike him and they were all drowned. The fourth flew to the heights where he has been ever since. In Central America, the bird Voc was the messenger of Hurakon, the tempest god of thunder and lightning. The Passamaquoddy told of his superiority over all others as the maker of wind, creator of storms and the source of thunder and lightning.

In general, he was a helper to man and a cultural hero to the culture gods of the Pacific as they were beholden to him for the things that he had taught man. Some people thought that he looked like an Eagle so is often seen in totems with a whale that was supposed to be his natural food. When the Thunderbird was hungry, he flew down to the sea, grabbed a whale in his talons and flew back to his mountain home. Whale bones have been found on mountain tops but never any Thunderbird bones!

Tinamous

These interesting birds are found from Mexico to Patagonia and range in size from a bantam chicken to a large rooster. They are usually gray or brown, streaked, barred or mottled with short tails and slender down-curved bills. The sexes look alike.

Throughout their range, they are hunted for food and sport. They are said to be the finest eating birds. The breast is chicken colored but tenderer, sweeter and even has more flavor!

Titmouse — Tit in Europe *4 1/2 - 6 1/2"*

This relative of our Chickadee got its name from the Icelandic "titr" and the English "mose" meaning small bird. The Tufted Titmouse *Parus bicolor* of this country is gray with a crest and black forehead. They are very active, curious and like bird-feeders and often hang upside down. People call them the "Peter-bird" from their call. In Germanic folklore, Tits were held in high esteem, sacred and prophetic. However, in the Low Countries they were said to be careless and gossips. They still have the affectionate name of "Tom Tit" and were made famous in Gilbert and Sullivan's "The Mikado" with a song of "Tit Willow, Tit Willow." The actual song of the Willow Tit is a far cry from that of the operetta!

Toucan

Toucans 4-25"

The thirty-five species of these varied sized birds are among the noisiest of the jungle dwellers of Central and South America. The native Tupi Indians called the bigger species "Toco" and the smaller ones "Arassaris" which were later changed to Toucan and Aracari. Their bills can be as large as their bodies and are extremely colorful and very light. They are fruit eaters and when they get out a piece, they throw their heads back to let it go down, likewise with water. They have a habit of folding themselves up as they sleep. They rest their bill on the center of the back and with a hinged-type tail cover it up. This spreads out over the shoulders so they resemble a ball!

Towhee, Eastern
Pipilo erythrophthalmus 8"

This male is rufous-sided with a black head and upper parts, white underparts, wing patches and tail corners while the female is brown where he is black. This coloring has resulted in people calling them "Ground Robins." They are slenderer and smaller than the Robin and are found from Canada to Central America. The Western form of this bird was formerly called the Spotted Towhee as both sexes have white spots above and two white wing bars. The Pueblo liked the white of their breast as to them it meant the West. Its long second scientific name means red-eyed. This garden bird has had a series of name changes from Red-eyed to Rufous-sided to Eastern but no change in its song of "drink your tea!"

Tropicbird, Red-tailed
Phaethon rubricauda 16-40"

These white birds with a few black markings on the wings and face have two central elongated tail feathers which gives them an extra foot in length. These pelagic seabirds are often called "Bos'n-bird" because their long tail feathers resemble marlin spikes. They seldom rest on water and are poor swimmers. They fed mainly on fish and squid for which they dive fifty feet or more from the air with half closed wings. After a small splash, they shake off the water and fly again. The natives of the South Seas valued their tail feathers for ornamental use and gathered them by pulling them out of nesting birds so as not to harm them and let them grow in again. Their white breast feathers were used in the beautifully woven capes of the former Hawaiian chiefs. The name "Tropicbird" came about as sailors never saw them beyond the tropical Atlantic, Pacific and Indian Oceans. The generic name *Phaethon* meaning Son of the Sun God, applies to the three species as they follow the sun and live in warm climes.

Trumpeter *Psophia crepitans 18"*

There are three species of these sociable birds of northeastern South America who have strident voices, long legs and neck and a short fowl-like beak. Their plumage is soft and dark but they have weak wings so run when in danger but they can swim! The natives kept them as watch-birds with their poultry. They do not breed well in captivity but are mighty good eating.

The Arawak of British Guiana had a tale of a great flood but no ark. The world was being engulfed by water and the only land left was a hilltop with tall coconut palms. The Heavenly leader, Sigu, sent all the animals and birds there. Those who could took to the trees and the rest were sealed in a cave with watertight wax. They were given a thorn to pierce the wax when they thought that all was well again. It was during this period that howler monkeys learned how to howl! They dropped coconuts until there was no longer a splash but a thud. The "Agami" or Trumpeter was in such a hurry to get down and find food that he was attacked by an army of starving ants coming out of their half-drowned nest. They swarmed all over his legs and ate all the flesh off so that is why he has spindle legs today!

Turacos in general *15-25"*

These twenty-two relatives of the Cuckoo, living in Africa, are called Plantain-eaters as it is their favorite food. Some of them are gray, brown and white and are called "Go-away birds." The others have green and blue coloring and red marked wings. Most bright colors in birds are from the refraction of tiny feather structures. However, in these birds the red and green are true pigments. The red is called "turacin" and is soluble and if a feather is put in a glass of water it will fade. In the heavy jungle though, they do not lose their color. Museum specimens get darker with age from the copper in the turacin as it oxidizes.

Turaco, Hartlaubi's *Tauraco hartlaubi 18"*

The Kenyan tribe of the Kikuyu, at the turn of the century, had a weird custom. Once a year, young women were compelled to wear a feather from this bird in their hair and forced to obey the wishes of the first young man that they met!

Turkey, Wild
Meleagris gallopavo male 48" female 36"

Fossils of these birds have been found dating from eleven million years ago. The name Turkey is a misnomer as they come from the Southwestern United States and Mexico and not from Turkey. They are the largest game bird native to the United States. They have a dark iridescent body, spurred legs, a red wattle (males) and a bare head. Their toes have a rudimentary webbing to them. They feed on insects, seeds, nuts and acorns and are birds of the open forests. Their scientific name *Meleagris* came from the legendary hero of the Caledonian Boar Hunt called Meleager. These birds were often confused with the Guinea Fowl. Their clucking noise of "turk, turk, turk" may have helped in their naming. In the 16th century, in England, they were known as the "Turkie-fowl" and a favorite of King Henry the VIII.

One of the first references to this bird came in 1519 "when Ambassador of Montezuma gave Cortez presents including six gold turkeys richly worked." Some of these live birds were taken by Herando Cortez back to Europe after his 16th century expedition to Mexico.

They were probably first domesticated in Mexico where they were used for food. They spread northward to the Southwest where the natives kept them for their feathers to use in decorations, to eat and to make whistles out of their bones. Some tribes thought that the Turkey helped in the creation of the world and showed people how to raise corn and other crops. Other tribes thought differently saying that they were sorcerers turned Turkey to prowl around at night and look for trouble. The Plains tribes replaced the Eagle with the Turkey in their fertility rites. Several tribes wore Turkey feathers woven into their garments.

Their spurs were used as arrow points and the quills from their large wing feathers were used to fletch the shaft of arrows. The Pueblo and Mayan peoples said that they were symbolic of rain.

They were abundant when the Pilgrims landed until about the time of the Revolutionary War. Their primary wing feathers were used as quills by the Colonists. Once they sold for one or two cents a pound and when the woods vanished so did the Turkeys. Now they have been reintroduced into several areas and are doing well.

As mentioned under House Sparrow, these pest birds carry a protozoan that kills Turkeys while they remain immune. "Talking Turkey" means getting down to the facts and no foolishness. "Strutting like a Turkey" shows self importance. "A Turkey" is a show that has flopped. The "Turkey Dance" is a non-sacred imitation of how a Turkey walks. The head is thrust forward and wagged from side to side and a toe to heel step is in an erratic course all to humorous music!

Turkey, Wild
Meleagris gallopavo race merriami male 48″ female 36″

These are sometimes called "Mountain Turkeys" and are one of the seven populations of Turkeys that are currently recognized. All of them are a sort of streamlined copy of the domesticated ones. The Pueblo felt that they represented the earth and were easy to domesticate. Their feathers were all of the "clothes" of the prayer-sticks and their neck feathers were used as fetishes. In the early times, cloaks were made out of their skins. They were not the overlapping type as the skins were twisted on the central fiber of the yucca plant in a spiral fashion and then tied together to make a mantle. They vary from the eastern form in having whitish tips to their tails instead of chestnut. They roam the mountains of Southern Colorado, New Mexico, Arizona and Western Texas.

Turnstone, Ruddy
Arenaria interpres 9 1/2"

These chunky, short-necked birds are closely related to Snipe and Plovers. They have bright chestnut and black coloring on their backs, are white below, with white heads and black chest bands. They are called "Calico-backs" from their back pattern named for Calicut in India where they make dappled patterned cloth. They are well named *Arenaria*, the Latin meaning "having to do with sand," as they turn over stones on the beaches and mud flats to find insects and marine life to eat. They like the tundra as they nest on all sides of the North Pole and winter on both coasts of the Atlantic and Pacific Oceans.

Umbrellabirds *Cephalopterus 16"*

These three black Crow-sized birds are tropical Cotingas. Their claim to fame is the fact that they can raise their crests over their heads to look like umbrellas. This is done when trying to attract females. To add to their odd heads, they have a lappet or wattle that hangs from the throat. In one species it can be thirteen inches and feathered. In the other, it is a bit shorter and in the third it is unfeathered and bright red! You can look for these fruit-eating birds in the tree tops of the jungles of Costa Rica down to Brazil.

Vulture, Bearded (Lammergeyer)
Gypaetus barbatus about 4'

These big birds are solitary and look more like a Falcon than a Vulture. They have pointed wings and a wing span of eight to ten feet. The word Vulture comes from the Latin "vultur" meaning to pluck or tear as in their food habits. Pliny described their custom of breaking bones of heavy shelled turtles by dropping them on rocks from up in the air. It seems that Aeschylus was supposed to have been killed by one such missile dropped by this bird who mistook his bald head for a rock! The poor man apparently had been forewarned by a message "a house falling on your head." These birds live in the remote mountains of Southern Europe, Africa and Central Asia but are rare throughout. The local peasants claimed that these birds were very fond of killing young lambs so were not popular.

Vulture, Black *Coragyps atratus 25"*

These birds are found in the southern parts of the United States and can be found as far south as Chile and Argentina. They have short broad wings that show white patches near the base of the primaries when they fly. Their tails are short and no longer than their feet. Their heads are gray and they have a labored flight compared to the Turkey Vulture. Like all Vultures they are carrion eating but will resort to killing sickly animals and nestlings of Herons and Egrets. They have an interesting (?) habit of defecating on their legs to cool them. This is a thermoregulatory technique known as urohydrosin!

Vulture, Egyptian
Neophron percnopterus 23-27"

They are a black and white Old World Vulture with a pointed head. Only their faces are bare and they are smaller than the other Vultures but the most numerous. They tend to live in mountain areas. In ancient Egypt, they represented Nekht, the tutelary deity of the south who appeared to man in that form and protected the queens of Egypt by wearing their Vulture head-dresses. They were called "Pharaoh's pets" or "Pharaoh's chickens." They were such good scavengers that they kept the streets clean so it was forbidden to harm one. They were the symbol of voracity, especially in the warm countries where carrion spoils fast. To the Jews, they were unclean. They were the bird of Ares, the Greek god of war and followed armies into battle to collect their prey, the fallen soldiers. The Roman augurs said that they laid thirteen eggs but used one to clean out the nest and it was thrown out. The Arabs were said to prick out the eyes of a dead one to extract the fluid and then paint their own eyes with it to see better!

Vulture, Turkey *Cathartes aura 26-32"*

These American Vultures soar in wide circles and seem to rock from side to side as they fly with few wing flaps. They look like Eagles with a six foot wing span. The adults have bare red heads and the young have black ones. They have excellent eyesight to locate dead animals to eat. It is just as well that their heads are bare of feathers since they only eat carrion.

The Apache liked them as they could watch them sail around and then locate a wounded deer. In Louisiana, they said

Turkey
Vulture

the reason they got bald was because a pan of hot ashes was thrown at the Vulture's head in revenge for an injury that the bird had done to a rabbit! The Iroquois said that originally all the birds were naked and asked for coverings. In those days they could talk to each other and were wiser than humans. Finally, they persuaded the Vulture to make the long journey to get them clothes. He was a clean bird when he left but en route he ate a lot of filth. When he arrived at his destination, he carefully picked out the most beautiful for himself. Alas, he could not fly or soar in that lovely outfit so ended up as he is today. In spite of this, he did bring back feathers for the other birds.

Some tribes thought that he was one of the Golden Eagle's chief helpers. His job was to keep the earth clean and all the refuse from above and below the earth was his and he was very faithful in this task. In Mexico, the natives had their own version of the Ark story. The first bird let out was a Vulture and he found carrion and never came back. Next out was the Hummingbird and he came back with a leaf so all was well. The Nebraska Winnebago had a tale of how once several water spirits were shot with arrows and they could not be extracted. They called on the Turkey Vulture who knew all about plants and roots and was a doctor. He found the answer. A shooter had killed a Vulture and had arrayed himself in his skin and had shot the spirits. As a result, the "Turkey Buzzard" became a good healer. The Pueblo felt that this bird had purifying and cleansing power as he was a scavenger. To some other tribes, he was a powerful medicine man able to get rid of evil, make contact with the dead or give blessings to the living. Much as he was admired, his feathers were never used in prayer-sticks because of his eating habits.

There are several sayings connected with this bird. If one sails around with little flapping, then the weather ahead would be nice but a lot of flapping meant rain. If you saw a lone bird then an unexpected guest was coming. Make a wish before it moved its wings and it would come true. If you saw its shadow and not the bird, it stood for illness and death so be sure not to let its shadow fall on you. Buzzard grease cured small pox and a little bag of feathers around the neck of a teething child would bring relief. Burn two feathers under the nose of a fainting person or one with an epileptic fit and they would be cured. Try hanging some bones around your neck to cure a headache.

In the South, they claimed that when these birds are seen in good numbers after the winter, there would be no more frost and it was safe to plant your crops. Hinckley, Ohio, announces the arrival of spring when these birds return. They call themselves "The Buzzard City." This seems like a questionable honor!

Wagtail *Moticilla 7"*

They come in combinations of yellow, white, gray and black. The have long wings and long tails that they are constantly wagging - hence their name. They live in the temperate parts of Eurasia, Africa, Southeast Asia and occasionally turn up in Alaska.

The Ainu of Japan said that the earth was once barren and uninhabitable. The Creator sent the Wagtail to trample the mud and beat it down with its feet. Slowly, it hardened and became elevated in spots so that the water drained away leaving good soil. As a result, they held this bird high in their esteem. The French peasants have an amusing tale of how this bird acquired his long tail. He borrowed the Wren's tail to go to the wedding of the Lark and never returned it. This is why he has to constantly wag it to make sure that it is still there.

A Welsh story tells of how Merlin ordered all birds to work on digging a water course. The Wagtail refused as he did not want to dirty his nice white legs. Therefore, he was condemned to have black legs, drink out of puddles and gutters and sing before it rained. There is another reason why he wags his tail. It is the fact that he had two drops of the devil's blood on it and cannot seem to shake them off!

Wallcreeper *Tichodroma muraria 6 1/2"*

These birds inhabit the mountains of central Eurasia to the Himalayas. They climb the rocky cliffs to get insects with their long down-curved bills. The mountaineers called them "Butterfly-birds" from their flight that is halting and butterfly-like. People said that they inhabited old cemeteries and nested in human skulls and the French even called them "Oiseau des cimetieres" referring to just that thought. They actually nest in holes and crannies between rocks. They have startling red wing coverts that were said to have been taken from the Cardinal's robes.

Warbler, Prothonotary
Protonotaria citrea 6 1/2"

These dark-eyed yellow birds are the most colorful of the few Warblers who nest in holes in trees. They are found in the Central, Eastern and Southern parts of the United States. Their name comes from the Greek-Latin word for scribe. They were named by the Catholic Louisiana Creoles in honor of the Papal Secretary who wore brilliant orange-yellow robes.

Warbler, Yellow *Dendroica petechia 5"*

This entirely yellow bird is well named. The male has small rusty streaks on his breast. They frequent wet habitats, woodlands and orchards from Alaska to Peru. They vary in intensity of color from area to area and there are several subspecies. To the Pueblo, the color yellow stood for the North and Northeast. It was also the color of pollen so they could use the feathers from these birds in their prayer-sticks.

Waxwing, Cedar *Bombycilla cedorum 7"*
Bohemian Waxwing *Bombycilla garrulus 8"*

Both of these birds can be found in North America. The Cedar Waxwing goes into South America while the Bohemian Waxwing is a bird of the Northwest. It also inhabits Northern Eurasia but not Bohemia for which it was named! They are both flock birds, have a high lisp and are sleek brown with a definite crest. They eat flower petals in the spring while waiting for their favorite food which is fruit to mature. When the berries are ripe they often tend to overeat, get drunk and then you can find them very relaxed under the cherry trees! It is interesting to note that they feed their young exclusively on insects.

The name Waxwing comes from the bright red waxy material often found on the tip of the adult's secondary wing feathers. They both have yellow tips to their tails which gives rise to their name of "Silky-tail." The Bohemian is larger and does not have the yellow on the belly or the white under the tail. They are grayer and have rusty tail underparts. As both of these species are irregular visitors and late nesters, they were looked upon as harbingers of war, the plague and death!

Wheatear *Oenanthe oenanthe 6"*

They are Thrushes of the open country and found in Eurasia, Labrador, Baffin Island, Greenland, Iceland and Alaska and winter in Africa. They occasionally wander southward into the States. They have black facial markings, black on the wings and tail and a white rump. They are a restless ground sparrow-like bird who flit from rock to rock, bobbing and fanning out their tails.

They get their name from the time of the wheat harvest when these birds are very plump and also from the Anglo-Saxon word for "white arse!" They used to be trapped and kept from the end of July to the end of September. They were well fed and most highly prized for food and they brought in good money. In Northern England and Scotland, they were supposed to foretell the death of a viewer if seen standing on a rock. If it was seen on grass or turf, then it meant good luck. Poor bird, as it loves rocks!

Whimbrel *Numenius phaeopus 17"*

This common European Curlew has the usual long curved bill, striped crown and is much smaller than the **Curlew** *Numenius arquata* 22". The Whimbrel in North America is a sub-species of this bird and was formerly called the Hudsonian Curlew. The cry of this bird is supposed to sound like the whimpering of the hounds hence its name, a corruption of "whimper-el." They were said to be the "Seven Whistlers" or "Gabriel's Hounds." In Leicestershire, England, no miner would go into a pit after hearing its call until a little time had passed. Their call was said to be a warning of an accident. They migrate low and on dark nights, so their sound was said to be unearthy and the Scots called them "Corpse-hounds."

Whip-Poor-Will
Caprimulgus vociferus 9 3/4"

These birds are mottled gray-brown all over with large eyes, a tiny bill with rectile bristles with which to catch and hold insects, and have very short legs. They prefer the mixed woodlands of the East and the mountain woodlands of the Southwest.

All members of the *Caprimulgidae* family tend to be thought of as birds of ill omen, misfortune and death. This is based on their nocturnal habits, along with some imagination, such as being messengers of death calling one spirit to join another in the next world.

Though usually thought of as bad luck birds, some people thought differently. The Ute of Colorado, said that they were the birds of the night and made the moon by magic by transforming a frog into it! The Iroquois said that moccasin flowers *Cypripedium* were their shoes. The mountaineers of the Southern Alleghenies said that the number of times it called would tell you the number of years it would be before you got married. Its appearance in the spring to the Winnebago meant that the danger of frost was over so they could plant their corn.

Many tribes imitated its cry as a means of communication in their wars. When you first hear it call in spring, it is telling you that you will be in the same place, doing the same thing on the same day next year! So make a wish and it will come true. How about this one? If you have a bad back and hear the Whip-Poor-Will calling, then turn somersaults timed to the bird's calling and your back problems will go away! John Burroughs, the naturalist, is reported to have had the record of hearing a bird call 1088 times in succession. They call about one second apart!

White-eye *Zosterops 4 1/2" - 6 1/2"*

This scientific name is from the Greek words for White-eye or Silver-eye and is pronounced with long vowels. These little birds of the Old World, Asia, the Islands of the Pacific and Indian Oceans, all have a conspicuous ring of white feathers around their eyes. The amount varies in the different species who can live side by side and not intermingle. Most people lump the twelve genera into Zosterops. These nectar-feeding birds stay in flocks except when nesting and have been good island hoppers. They vary in color from olive-green to gray-brown above to yellow, gray and white below. Generally, they have slender, pointed, down-curved bills for nectar, rounded wings and short legs. The sexes are alike and they divide the nesting chores.

Willet *Catoptrophorus semipalmatus 15"*

In Florida, they call this bird the "Christmas bird" just as they do the Black-bellied Plover, as that is when they arrive for the winter. They are found in North and South America. Their call sounds a bit like their name. They can be told by their gray back and heavily mottled appearance. They have a definite black and white wing pattern that is seen best when in flight. They are the only seashore Tattler that will perch on wires or telephone poles like the inland Upland Sandpiper (Plover)!

Woodcock *Scolopax rusticola 14"*

Their name is derived from the Anglo-Saxon word "cocc." They are often called "Cock of the woods" as they perform a remarkable twilight flight in the mating season. The male makes a sort of "peent" sound on the ground and then suddenly takes off into the sky. There he circles around with a twittering sound and then zooms down next to the female with a buzzing noise made by the air rushing through his wings and tail. He repeats this several times. They are a solitary woodland and wetlands bird who are larger than a Snipe and live in temperate Eurasia. There they were taken in nets or trapped for eating. They were extolled for their flavor as the "Dyetary" of 1542 said "a Woodcock is a meat of good temperance."

Woodcock, American *Scolopax minor 11"*

This bird does the amazing mating routine like his relative above and looks like him. They are cryptic in coloration with a barred head, long bill, large head with big eyes set way back. They are chunky, short-necked and legged and have rounded wings. They are solitary, nocturnal and secretive birds found in the wet woodlands of the East and South of North America. The Seneca thought that this bird, often called "Timber-doodle," was made out of the left over parts from other birds. They look like a dead leaf but were thought to be able to communicate via a fledged bird to the departed.

Woodpecker in general *3 1/2-24"*

Obviously, their name comes from their habits. They are good flyers but rarely go far from their vertical lives in trees. They have stiff tails for support and hard, straight pointed bills for chiseling in wood and bark. They have a long tongue that goes beyond the tip of the bill that has backward pointing barbs to secure the insects. Their skulls have thick walls to absorb the pounding by the powerful muscles in their thin necks. Their toes are two forward and two behind which helps in their tree-living habits. Most of them have loud voices. You can find them all over the world except in Australia, Madagascar and the Oceanic Islands.

Woodpeckers - European

One of these birds watched over Romulus and Remus according to Plutarch. They were often called the "Gertrude bird" because of this legend from Northern Europe. It seems that St. Peter and Jesus were hungry so asked old Gertrude for some bannock. She took a small piece but it grew too big in the skillet. She tried two other times with even smaller pieces with the same result. She would not part with any so the two men left. She was punished for her selfishness by becoming smaller and smaller and finally went up the chimney as a Woodpecker. Her back got blackened by the soot but her white apron remained as did her red hat. Several Woodpeckers answer that description. She found it hard to get food from the tree barks and rainwater. There are several similar versions and have been applied to Owls, Cuckoos and Lapwings.

Zeus, Mars and even Indra, from Hindu mythology, were transformed into Woodpeckers when they wanted to have a little fun! This made the early Christians identify these birds with the devil. Many people thought of them as rain birds and birds of thunder from their loud pecking noises. Woodpeckers were supposed to laugh before it rained to make all the insects come out of hiding so these birds could eat them. In Scandinavia, peasants thought if their cries were low and monotonous that the weather would be fine. If they were loud, then it meant storms and rain. They did not figure out that different Woodpeckers make different amounts of noise when pecking! If their call was near your home it could be a really bad sign. However, if you used the beak of a Woodpecker to get honey out of a hive, you would never be stung!

Woodpeckers from other areas

The Pueblo said that its drumming meant rain but also thunder which would eventually bring rain. The Dakota said that if a Woodpecker nested near a field that it was sacred so no one could touch its eggs as that would cause rain. However, if the Woodpecker nested away from the field, then it could be robbed by starving tribe members. The Navajo said that if it tapped on the logs of a hogan, it meant ill omen. The Winnebago considered Woodpeckers to be gossip birds. The Ainu of Japan said that it was the boatmaker's bird as it pecked out wood the same way that they did to make their dugout canoes!

Woodpecker, Green _Picus viridis 12"_

This green-backed, yellow-rumped Woodpecker can be found from Europe and Asia south to Borneo and Java. In the forest of Eurasia, they inhabit the same niche as the **Flicker** _Colaptes auratus_ in North America. Like them, they are ant eaters. They seem to laugh more than making the usual drumming noise. In the early Roman days, they were used for divination of the future.

Woodpecker, Ivory-billed
Campephilus principalis 20"

These black and white, red-crested Woodpeckers were formerly widespread in the mature forests of North America and Cuba. The cutting of big trees everywhere led to their demise. They are now listed as extinct. To the Natives of Vancouver Island, this bird was a real bringer of rain.

Woodpecker, Pileated
Dryocopus pileatus 16"

This is the biggest North American Woodpecker to be seen today. It has a black body and wings, white chin and a red crest. The male had a red mustache. The holes they make are oval or rectangular and they like the carpenter ants of dead and decaying wood. Because of their size, they were known to many natives as "Lord God Woodpecker."

Woodpecker, Red-bellied
Melanerpes carolinus 10"

These birds have a black and white barred back and a red nape. The male gets the red on his head as well. Their red belly is really a yellow-pink tinge. This southern North American bird is extending its range northward and is fond of feeding stations. To the Omaha, it was a special god. It is the guardian of the children as they kept their young in a safe place: a hole in a tree!

Woodpecker, Red-headed
Melanerpes erythrocephalus 10"

These black and white birds with startling red heads are found in the woodlands of temperate North America. They are getting quite rare in the northeast due to habitat loss and Starlings taking over their nesting sites. They can dig in the bark for insects but also catch them on the wing. They are also fond of berries, fruits and bird feeders.

Their habit of eating corn, fruit, berries and insects, got them into trouble in the seventeen hundreds. Some of the Colonies offered up to two pence apiece for each head. This was because of a debate as to whether they were good by eating harmful insects or bad because they ate fruit and hurt lumber. It wasn't until 1911 that the problem was officially settled. They were judged to be a good bird!

The Chitimacha of Northern Louisiana said that when the Great Deluge came, this bird went into the sky and hung on by his claws to escape drowning. However, its tail hung down into the muddy waters and so was stained black. According to the Ojibway, its red head came because of its prowess. They claimed that these red feathers were symbols of valor and were used on warrior's pipes. Their culture hero was told by this bird to shoot his last arrow at the scalp of his enemy. This he did and put the blood on the Woodpecker's head, so he has had a red head ever since. In Lower Missouri, the natives said that it was a great sorcerer. It could be a bird or a red man with a mantle or cloak over his arm. It could be grateful and even useful depending on its mood. It sometimes bored holes in the heads of enemies while they slept. Then it put maggots in the hole to cause the victims to be restless and crazy! That is not all. This bird made a bat out of a rat and a bird! The Pawnee said that they were the interpreters of Tirawa, the chief god, and these birds understood thunder. Sons of the chiefs wore caps of the head of this bird to show that they were under the protection of Tirawa.

Henry David Thoreau even dined on these birds according to his "Maine Woods." It must have been a pretty small meal unless he had a lot of them!

Wren *Troglodytes troglodytes (Winter Wren in North America) 4"*

These small birds with loud voices are called Jenny or Kitty Wren in Great Britain but in Holland and Germany they are considered males. Whatever sex they may be, Wren comes from the Anglo-Saxon word "wraenna" which was also used to mean lascivious! The French call them "Troglodyte mignon," also male, and meaning cave-dweller and this stems from its scientific name. This is probably because they make a large covered nest and sulk and roost among the roots and rocks. These little brown birds have slender sharp pointed bills, cock their tails up over the back and live close to the ground.

This Wren turns up in all sorts of literature and in all kinds of situations. One of the most famous myths was when all the birds gathered to decide who would be the King of the Birds. They decided that the winner would be the one who could fly the highest. They all tried but the Eagle was the winner. He was about to be declared the King of the birds, when off his back flew the Wren. Another time, the Wren flew up into the sky to get fire and in so doing burned off all her feathers and arrived back naked. All the birds gave her a feather except the Owl who refused. The Owl and the Wren met again when all the birds were getting tired of the Wren's antics. They put her in jail with the Owl as her jailer, while they decided on what punishment should be levied against the Wren. Well, the Owl fell asleep and the Wren escaped so that is why, through shame, you rarely see an Owl by day.

In some parts of Europe, it was said to be the pet of the Virgin Mary and in other areas it was in league with the devil. The Greeks said that it was unlucky to see one at a wedding as the male makes several nests. True! The Irish had a saying "the Robin and the Wren are God's two Holy Men."

For centuries a most interesting event took place. It was called the "Wren Hunt" or "the Hunting of the Wren." It took place in the South of France, Wales and the Celtic parts of England and Ireland. It took place between Christmas Eve and Twelfth Night. The custom died out around the time of World War I. It was an ancient practice carrying out a religious or symbolic idea, the meaning of which has been lost in antiquity. Basically, it went as follows. A group of men and boys would capture a Wren, either killing it or maiming it, and tied it to a post or put it in a special box. This, they carried around the village chanting songs and asking for alms. At the end of the day they would bury it with all due reverence. We know that the Druids drew auguries from the chirping of the Wren. Maybe the early Christians objected to the Druid use and so condemned it as a symbol of heathen rites. They may have encouraged their converts to kill this bird around the Christmas season to lessen the Druid influence. The day on which the Hunt took place varied from one area to another. It was said that St. Stephen was about to escape his execution, when a Wren alighted on the jailer's face and awakened him. On the Isle of Man, on New Year's Day, they sought out the Wren to collect its feathers. This is because the bird turned itself into a lovely siren-mermaid and lured sailors to their watery graves, and then escaped as a Wren. So on New Year's Day, it is hunted, killed and its feathers distributed as talisman against any future ship wrecks. Wrens were not liked in Ireland because they said that when the Irish were fighting Cromwell's army, the Wrens came and pounded on the drums of the sleepy soldiers. This awakened them and they slaughtered the Irish.

The British tradition had it that the Wren was the Robin's

brother, but in Iceland she was the mouse's brother. The Norse people said she was a malignant fairy who led youths astray. She turns up in stories of witchcraft, sorcery and even immortality and was often painted with the Robin and the Raven in the company of saints! In France, they believed that the Wren, Lark, Swallow and Robin were fire bringers and as such were sacred. Robbing their nests was a sin and punishment came to the offenders by their houses burning down. Added to this, was the fact that the offender's fingers would shrivel up and fall off.

There were "Wrens" in World War II, the Women's Royal Naval Volunteer Service. The people who thought up the name must have overlooked the fact that in the Crimean War, a camp follower was called a "Wren" and lived in the bush! The Wren was quite a bird!

Wrens in general in North America

They are easy to recognize as they are similar in appearance with the sexes looking alike. They have slender bills and up tilted tails. They come in brown and gray and are striped, spotted or streaked with brown, gray, black or white. They are from four to eight and a half inches but most are small. The nine species found here are chunky in form, inquisitive and noisy.

The Pawnee said that it was a laughing bird and the god of happiness because it sang so exuberantly. Lots of people thought that if it built a nest near your house that good luck would follow. The Cherokee said that the Wren was a busybody and got up early in the morning to bring the news to the council of birds. When a new baby was born, she reported its sex. If a boy, they would all sing in mournful chorus "alas, the whistle of the arrow. My skin will burn." They assumed that the boy would use arrows on them and then roast them on a stick. If the child was a girl they all sang happily "thanks, the sound of the pestle. At her home I shall surely be able to scratch where she sweeps." This meant when the girl made corn meal, they would be able to pick up a few crumbs.

Wren, Canyon *Salpinctus mexicanus 5 3/4"*

This western bird is brown with a white throat. It inhabits canyons and cliffs near the water and is non-migratory. The scientific name *Salpinctus* is Greek for trumpeter. The natives considered its great voice to stand for the War Chief, one of the town criers. Its voice can echo and fool an enemy so they used its feathers on their prayer-sticks.

Wren, House *Troglodytes aedon 4 3/4"*

This noisy wren lives from Canada to Tierra del Fuego. It is sort of a plain brown bird that lacks any special field markings. It has a longer tail than the Winter Wren (Wren in Europe) and has less barring on the breast. They are fond of birdhouses and if you put up several in a small area, they will be used. You will not have several families but just one as the male builds dummy nests in the others. They are not particular about the house but do need an opening about the size of a quarter. This will keep out the House Sparrows but not allow the male to bring in big twigs as they do sometimes. They are affectionately called Jenny Wren.

Wren

Wren, Rock *Salpinctus obsoletus 6"*

These western birds are grayish with a pale finely streaked breast and buffy tips to the tail. They are found from Canada to Costa Rica where they enjoy scrub land and semi-arrid areas. They bob their heads frequently especially when excited. The Pueblo thought that they were crazy fliers and so would do anything to confuse the enemy. If you touched one you might go crazy. In spite of this, they used their feathers as fetishes!

Wryneck *Jynx torquilla 7"*

This temperate Eurasian bird has a habit of twisting its neck, hence the name. It is an insect eating bird but picks up food on the surface and does not bore for it. Their tails are soft unlike their relatives the Woodpeckers. This odd Woodpecker was used as an engraving on amethyst and set in gold as a love charm. The wings and feet were spread out upon a wheel so as to form four spokes. This magical wheel, when spun with the proper incantations, had strong powers and was used to recover unfaithful lovers!

Xenops, Plain   *Xenops minutus 5"*

This bird is a member of the Ovenbird family called *Furnariidae*. They are not related to the Ovenbird of the Wood Warbler family. They are one of the most diverse and drab colored bird families. They range from Mexico to Brazil and Paraguay. This bird being only five inches in size is one of the smallest as some others reach eleven inches. It has a strange upcurved bill which gives it the name of "Recurved-bill." It hops and hitches along sideways not using its bill for support. It clings as do Tits in odd positions in order to obtain their insect food. Most of this family make a sort of covered nest, the source of their name Ovenbirds. This little fellow is a nonconformist and nests in one inch holes made by other birds.

Yellowhammer   *Emberiza citrinella 8 1/2"*

These are a common Eurasian bird with a streaked yellow head on a brownish body and has a chestnut rump. They can be told by their white outer tail feathers and their habitat of open country. Their song is usually translated as "little-bit-of-bread-and-and-no——cheese" all in a monotone. The word hammer is a corruption of the German word "ammer" meaning a Bunting. They belong in this family. The eggs of these birds are spotted red because the birds were said to have fluttered around the Cross, so as a result they have blood marks on them. In Denmark, a sufferer from jaundice would eat Yellowhammer feathers and bones so as to be cured. Glug! It is interesting to note that yellow is the color of the quarantine flag!

Yellowthroat *Geothlypis trichas 5"*

This Warbler has a yellow throat (well named), and a black facial mask (males only), a white belly and tan sides. They live from Canada to the West Indies and Panama. They have a very distinctive song of "witchity, witchity, witchity, witch" or a variation of same. According to the Pueblo, this Wren-like bird's yellow color stood for pollen and so they were considered the bringer of spring.

Zosterops see White-eye

Zosterops means girdled appearance which refers to their eye-rings. I have included this name for three reasons. First, they are amazing looking birds. Secondly, they have an intriguing scientific name and, lastly, I needed a Z!

White-eye

Bibliography

Ackworth, Bernard. "Bird and Butterfly Mysteries." London, Eyre and Spottiswode, 1955.

Allen, Glover. "Birds and their Attributes." Dover, 1962.

American School of Classical Studies at Athens. "Birds of the Athenian Agra." Princeton University Press, 1985.

Armstrong, E.A. "The Folklore of Birds." London, Collins, 1958.

———"The Life and Lore of the Bird." New York, Crown, 1975.

Aristophanes. "The Birds." 414 B.C.

Austin, Oliver L. Jr. "Birds of the World." New York, Golden, 1961.

———-"A Guide to Bird Classification - Families of Birds." New York, Golden, 1965.

Barlow, Virginia. "The Nature of the Islands, Plants and Animals of the Eastern Caribbean." Florida, Dunedin, Chris Doyle Pub., 1993.

Batcheler, Julia F. and Claudia de Lys. "Superstitions? Here's Why." New York, Harcourt Brace, 1954.

Bible, The Holy, 1611 known as the King James Version.

Borland, Hal. "Audubon Magazine." May and November 1974.

Bowes, Anne LaBastille. "Birds of the Mayas." New York, Big Moose, West of the Wind Pub., 1974.

Brewer, Rev. E. Cobham. "Dictionary of Phrase and Fable." Philadelphia, Lippincott.

Brown, W.J. "The Gods have Wings." London, Constable and Co., 1936.

Bruun, Bartel. "The Hamlyn Guide to Birds of Britain and Europe." London, Hamlyn, 1971.

Burland, Cottie. "North American Indian Mythology." New York, Hamlyn, 1973.

Campbell, Bruce and Elizabeth Lack. "Dictionary of Birds." Buteo Books for British Ornithologists' Union, 1985.

Caras, Roger. "Source of Thunder." Audubon Magazine 1972 v. 70 #6.

Choate, Ernest A. "The Dictionary of American Bird Names." Boston, Gambit, 1973.

Clarke, Helen A. "A Child's Guide to Mythology." New York, Bale and Taylor Co., 1908.

Clarke, "Totem of Birds of Australia."

───-"Totem of North American Indian."

DeKay, Charles. "Bird Gods." New York, A.S. Barnes, 1898.

deLys, Claudia. "A Treasury of American Superstitions." New York, Philosophical Society, 1948.

Douglas, Norman. "Birds and Beasts of the Greek Anthology." London, Chapman and Hall Ltd., 1928.

Drury, Roger W. and Samuel S. Drury. "In Pursuit of the Pelican." New Hampshire, Concord, Private pub., 1931.

Elliot, Daniel Giraud. "Game Birds of North America." New York, Harpers, 1897.

───-"Wild Fowl of North America." New York, Harpers, 1898.

Encyclopedia Americana. "American Mythology." vol. 1.

Evans, A.H. "Turner on Birds." England, Cambridge, 1903.

Falla, R.A., R.S. Gibson and E.G. Turbott. "The New Guide to the Birds of New Zealand and Outlying Islands." Auckland, Collins, 1979.

Fisher, James and R.T. Peterson. "The World of Birds." London, Macdonald, 1964.

Foster, Thomas. "Observations on the Natural History of Swallows." London, Redwood Press, 1972, 6th ed.

Frazer, Sir James George. "The New Golden Bough." abridgement ed. Dr. T.H. Gaster, New York, Criterion Books, 1959.

Friedereci, Peter. "Flashing Red," "Birder's World." 1994 v. 8, #6.

Friedmann, Herbert. "A Bestiary for St. Jerome." Washington, D.C. Smithsonian Institution, 1980.

Funk and Wagnall's. "Standard Dictionary of Folklore, Mythology, and Legend." Marion Leach ed. 2 vol. New York, 1951.

Garfield, Viola E. "Meet the Totem." Alaska, Sitka Printing Press, 1951.

Goldsmith, Oliver. "An History of Earth and Animated Nature." London, 1774.

——-"Natural History." London, abridged 1827.

Gotch, A.F. "Birds, Their Latin Names Explained." London, Dorset, Blandford Press, 1981.

Grant, Peter R. "Ecology and Evolution of Darwin's Finches." Princeton University Press, 1986.

Grieve, Symington. "The Great Auk or Garefowl." London and Edinburgh, Ballantyne Press, 1885.

Gross, Alfred. "The Heath Hen." Memoirs of the Boston Society of Natural History, vol. 6, #4, 1928.

Grossman, M.L. and John Hamlet. "Birds of Prey of the World." New York, Clarkson and Potter, 1964.

Gruson, Edward S. "Words for Birds." New York, Quadrangle Press, 1972.

——"Checklist of the World's Birds." New York, Quadrangle Press, 1976.

Gurney, J. "Early Annals of Ornithology." London, Whitherby, 1921.

Hardy, J. "Popular History of the Cuckoo." "Folklore Record," part 2 before 1885.

Harter, Walter. "Birds in Fact and Legend." New York, Sterling, 1979.

Harting, James E. "The Birds of Shakespeare." Chicago, Argment, 1965.

Harwood, Michael. "The View from Great Gull." New York, E. F. Dutton, 1976.

Hasell, Sandy. "Know the Navajo." Denver, 1936.

Heck, J.G. "Iconographic Encyclopedia of Science, Literature and Art." New York, Gerrigue, vol. 2, 1851.

Heron, Robert. "Elegant Extracts of Natural History." Edinburgh, MDCCXCII, vol. 2.

Hochbaum, H. Albert. "Travels and Traditions of Waterfowl." Minneapolis, Univ. of Minnesota Press, 1935.

Holmgren, Virginia C. "Bird Walk through the Bible." New York, Seabury Press, 1972.

——"The Way of the Hummingbird." California, Santa Barbara, Capra Press, 1986.

——"Owls in Folklore and Natural History." California, Santa Barbara, Capra Press, 1988.

Horsley, Canon J.W. "Some Folklore and Legends of Birds." New York, E.S. Gordon, 1914.

Hulme, F. Edward. "Natural History and Legend." London, Bernard Quartitch, 1895.

Ingersoll, Ernest. "Birds in Legend, Fable and Folklore." New York, Longmans Green and Co., 1923.

Iredale, Tom. "Birds of Paradise and Bower Birds." Australia, Melbourne, Georgian House, 1950.

Isler, Morton L. and Phyllis P. Isler. "The Tanagers." Washington, D.C. Smithsonian Institution Press, 1987.

Jackson, Jerome K. "Down the Hatch." Birder's World, v. 8:6, 1994.

Jameson, William. "The Wandering Albatross." New York, Doubleday, 1911.

Jipson, N.W. "Oologist" supplement. June 1, 1922.

Jobling, James A. "Dictionary of Scientific Bird Names." Oxford University Press, 1991.

Johnston, Johanna. "The Eagle in Fact and Fiction." Harlan Quist, Crown Pub., 1966.

King, Ben, M. Woodcock and E.C. Dickinson. "A Field Guide to the Birds of South-East Asia." London, Collins, 1976.

Kinnaird, Margaret F. "Indonesia's Hornbill Haven." Natural History, v. 105:1, 1996.

Kulpa, Jack. "The Rune of the Loon." Field & Stream, April 1996.

"Larousse World Mythology." Pierre Grimal, London, Hamlyn, 1965 ed.

Leach, Marion. "The Rainbow Book of American Folklore and Legend." New York, World Pub., 1958.

Ley, Willy. "Dawn of Zoology." New York, Prentice Hall, 1968.

"Life Treasury of American Folklore." New York, Life, Time ed. 1961.

Limburg, Peter. "What's-in-the-name-of Birds." New York, Coward, McCann and Geoghagan, 1975.

Lloyd, Lewis A.W. "Bird Facts and Fallacies." London, Hutchinson.

Lockley, R.M. "Puffins." New York, Doubleday Anchor, 1962.

Lutwach, Leonard. "Birds in Literature." Gainesville, Univ. of Florida, 1994.

McAtee, W.L. "Folklore of Birds." "Florida Naturalist," April, July and October, 1955.

Manry, David E. "Dipper Scavenger." "Birder's World," v. 8:6 1994.

Marrott, Alice and Carol K. Rechlin. "American Epic - the Story of the American Indian." New York, Putnam, 1969.

Mayr, Ernst. "Birds of the Southwest Pacific." New York, Macmillan, 1945.

Medlin, Faith. "Centuries of Owls." Ct. Norwalk, Silvermine Press, 1967.

"Meet the Totem." 1951.

Melancon, Claude. "Percé and Bonaventure Island Seabirds." Montreal, Le Edition du Jour.

Mercatante, Anthony E. "Zoo of the Gods." New York, Harper and Row, 1974.

Miles, Alfred H. "Natural History in Antidote." London, 189?.

National Geographic Society. "Field Guide to the Birds of North America." Washington, D.C., 1983.

New York State Bulletin #25. "Myths and Legends of the New York Iroquois." 1908.

Newton, Alfred. "A Dictionary of Birds." London, Adam and Charles Black, 1896.

Parmelee, Alice. "All the Birds of the Bible." New York, Harper and Row, 1959.

Perrins, C.M. and A.L.A. Middleton, editors. "Encyclopedia of Birds." New York, Facts on File, 1985.

Peterson, Roger Tory. "Symbols of Nature in Art." "Audubon Magazine," v. 43, 1941.

———"The Birds." Life Nature Library, Time Inc., 1963.

———"Field Guide to the Birds East of the Rockies." Boston, Houghton Mifflin, 1980.

———-"Field Guide to Western Birds." Boston, Houghton Mifflin, 1990.

———, G. Mountfort and P.A.D. Hollam. "Field Guide to the Birds of Britain and Europe." Boston, Houghtin Mifflin, 1966.

Potter, Stephen and Laurens Sargent. "Pedigree." New York, Taplinger, 1973.

"Primitive Americans." 1965.

Pycraft, W.P. "The Dictonary of Birds." New York, 1911.

Robbins, Chandler S.; Bertel Bruun and Herbert S. Zim. "A Guide to the Field Identification - Birds of North America." New York, Golden Press, 1966.

Rowland, Beryl. "Birds with Human Souls." Univ. of Tennessee Press, 1989.

Schulberg, Budd. "Swan Watch." New York, Delacorte Press, 1975.

Slater, Peter. "A Field Guide to Australian Birds." PA. Wynnewood, Livingston Pub. Co., v. 1 non-passerines, 1971.———-v. 2 passerines, Australia, Adelaide, Rigby, 1974.

Smith, Bosworth. "Bird Life and Bird Lore." London, John Murray, 1901.

Smith, Dick and Robert Easton. "California Condor - Vanishing American." CA. Charlotte/Santa Barbara, Menaty & Loftin, 1964.

Spence, Lewis. "The Myths of the North American Indians." New York, Stokes, 1914.

Spencer, Robert F. and Jesse D. Jennings, etc. "The Native Americans." New York, Harper and Row, 1965.

Stearns, Winifred A. "Labrador." Boston, 1884.

Stedman, David W. Article on the Passenger Pigeon. "New York Conversationist." April, 1996.

Stiles, F. Gary and Alexander F. Skutch. "Guide to the Birds of Costa Rica." New York, Cornell University, 1989.

Storer, Robert W. "The Resplendent Quetzal." "Birder's World." v. 8:6, 1994.

Stuart, Dorothy M. "The Book of Birds and Beasts." London, Meutheun & Co., 1957.

Swainson, Rev. Charles. "Provencial Names and Folklore of British Birds." London, English Dialect Society, 1885.

Swann, H. Kirke. "A Dictionary of English and Folklore Names of British Birds." London, Whitherby, 1913.

Terres, John K. "Birds Carried by Birds." "Canadian Audubon," v. 78:4, 1966.

——-"The Audubon Society Encyclopedia of North American Birds." New York, Knopf, 1980.

Thompson, D'Arcy W. "A Glossary of Greek Birds." Oxford, Claredon Press, 1895.

Thompson, A. Landsborough. "A New Dictionary of Birds." London, British Ornithologists' Union and Nelson, 1964.

Ticehurst, N.F. "The Mute Swan in England." London, Cleaver and Hume Press, 1957.

Trumbull, Gordon. "Names and Portraits of Birds." New York, Harpers, 1888.

Tyler, Hamilton A. "Pueblo Birds and Their Myths." Univ. of Oklahoma Press, 1979.

"U.S.A. Today" for March 28, 1995.

U.S. Dept. of the Interior. "Birds in Our Lives." Alfred Stefferod ed., 1966.

Vinycomb, John. "Fictitious and Symbolic Creatures in Art." London, 1906.

Walker, Margaret Coulson. "Bird Legend and Life." New York, Baker and Taylor, 1908.

Wallace, George J. and H.V. Mahan. "An Introduction to Ornithology." New York, Macmillan, 1975.

Welker, Robert H. "Birds and Men." New York, Atheneum, 1966.

Weltfish, Gene. "The Lost Universe - the Way of Life of the Pawnee." Basic Books, 1971.

Wetmore, Alexander. "The Migration of Birds." Cambridge, Harvard Univ. Press, 1930.

White, Gilbert. "The Illustrated Natural History of Selborne." New York, St. Martin's Press, 1981.

White, T.H. "The Bestiary." New York, Putnam, 1960.

Williams, Jay. "The Fall of the Sparrow." New York, Oxford, 1951.

Woodcock, Martin. "Collins Guide to the Birds of the Indian Subcontinent." London, 1980.

Woodcock, P.G. "Short Dictionary of Mythology." New York, Philosophical Society, 1953.

Yapp, Brysdon. "Birds in Medieval Manuscripts." British Library Board, 1961.

Appendix

Aelainus, early 2nd. century A.D., author.

Aeschylus, 525-456, Greek dramatist.

Aesop, c. 620-560 B.C., Fablist.

Aldrovanus, Aldrovandi Ulisse, 1522-1605., Renaissance scientist, physician.

Alexander the Great, ruled Persia 336-323, died 323 B.C. pupil of Aristotle.

Anderson, Hans Christian, 1805-1875, Danish author of fairy tales.

Anne of Cleves, 1515-1557, 4th. wife of Henry VIII.

Anne, Queen of England, 1675-1714.

Anthony, Saint, died 357 A.D. an Egyptian.

Apollo, Greek god of love.

Aristophanes, c. 448-380 B.C., Greek dramatist.

Aristotle, 384-322 B.c., Greek philosopher, historian, naturalist.

Arthur, King, Medieval legendary king of the quest for the Holy Grail.

Athene, Greek mythological goddess of wisdom, war, art and the night.

Attila the Hun, died 453 B.C. Warrior King of the Huns.

Audubon, John James, 1785-1851, French/U.S. famous bird painter and author.

Augustine, Saint 354-430 A.D., famous son of a heathen father.

Augustus, 27 B.C. - 14 A.D. Roman ruler.

Aurelius, Roman ruler 270 B.C.

Becket, Thomas a, 1118-1170. Martyr, Archbishop of Canterbury, murdered.

Benedict, Saint, 480-543, Founder of Benedictine Order.

Bewick, Thomas, 1753-1828, British naturalist, author, artist.

Boleyn, Anne, c.1507-1536, 2nd. wife of Henry VIII, mother of Queen Elizabeth the First.

Brennus, 4th. century leader of the Gauls.

Buddha, 563-480 B.C.

Buffon, George le Clerc, Comte de Buffon, 1707-1788, French author, naturalist.

Burroughs, John, 1837-1921, U.S. naturalist, author.

Caesar, Julius, 100-44 B.C., Roman general.

Cajun, descendants of French-Canadians driven out of Nova Scotia by the British, settling in Louisiana 1700s.

Calvert, Lord Baltimore, c. 1580-1632, English Baron who founded a New World Colony, later Maryland.

Cartier, Jacques, 1491-1557, French explorer of Canada and the St. Lawrence River 1534.

Catesby, Mark, 1731-1774, British naturalist, author "Natural History of the Carolinas".

Charlemagne or Charles the Great, 742-814, French King.

Charlevoix, Pierre Francois Xavierde, 1682-1761, French Jesuit who explored Canada.

Chaucer, Geoffroy, 1340-1400, English author of "Canterbury Tales".

Churchill, Winston S., 1874-1965, British Prime Minister, 1940-45, 1951-55.

Cicero, Marcus Tullius, 106-43 B.C., Roman statesman, scholar, writer.

Clark, William, 1770-1838, U.S. surveyor, naturalist, collector.

Cleopatra VII, 69-30 B.C. Queen of Egypt, Lover of Julius Caesar and later of Mark Anthony, last of the Ptolemy rulers.

Columbus, Christopher, 1451-1506, Italian explorer for Spain, discovered the New World 1492.

Coloridge, Samuel Taylor, 1772-1834, English poet.

Cook, Captain James, 1718-1779, English explorer, navigator.

Cortez, Hernando, 1485-1547, Spaniard conquered Mexico 1519.

Crivelli, Carlo, c. 1430/35 - 1493/95. Italian painter.

Cuthburt, Saint d.687, English monk missionary.

Daigo, 885-930, 60th. Emperor of Japan.

Darwin, Charles Robert, 1809-1882, British naturalist, wrote "The Origin of Species" after his "Beagle" voyage.

David, King died 926 B.C. United Israel with Jerusalem as capital, ruled 37 years.

Delius, Frederick, 1862-1934, English composer.

Druids, an order of priests, teachers, philosophers, astronomers of ancient Gaul and Britain, used human sacrifices.

Edward the Confessor, 1002-1066, English king.

Edward I, 1239-1307, English king.

Edward II, 1284-1327, English king.

Edward III, 1312-1377, English king.

Edward, The Black Prince, son of Edward III, Prince of Wales, famous for his black armour, fierce fighting, ostrich plumes, one of the original Knights of the Garter.

Edwards, George, 1743-1760, English painter, art works in "Gleanings of Natural History"

Elijah the Tishbite, Prophet from I Kings.

Elizabeth I, 1534-1607, Queen of England.

Elliott, Daniel Giraud, 1835-1915, U.S. ornithologist, author.

Francis the First, 1494-1547, English king.

Francis of Assisi, Saint, 1182-1266, associated with nature, founder of the Franciscans.

Franklin, Benjamin 1706-1790, U.S. statesman, diplomat, inventor.

Frederick of Brandenberg, 1620-1688.

Gaelic, old Irish language.

George V, 1860-1936, King of England.

Gilbert, William S., 1836-1911, English lyricist of Gilbert & Sullivan operettas.

Grant, Peter R., Ornithologist, presently Professor Princeton University, authority with wife Rosemary on Darwin's Finches.

Grant, General Ulyssus S., 1742-86, led Union Army in U.S. Civil War.

Harold, died 1040, son of King Canute.

Henry III, 1207-72, King of England.

Henry IV, 1366-1413. King of England.

Henry IV, known as Henry of Navarre, 1553-1610, First of the Bourbon kings of France.

Henry VIII, 1491-1547, much married King of England.

Herodotus, c.484-420 B.C., Greek historian.

Hochbaum, H. Albert, 1911-1988c., Canadian author, painter.

Humboldt, Freidrick Wilhelm Karl Heinrich Alexander, Baron de Humboldt, 1769-1859, German scientist, explorer.

Ibycus, 6th. century poet.

Inuit means "The People" as opposed to Eskimo which means
"They eat raw flesh".

James I, 1561-1625, Son of Mary, Queen of Scots, King of England.

Jefferson, Thomas, 1743-1826, Third President of U.S.

Jerome, Saint, 341-420.

John the Baptist, Saint, born 5 B.C., wrote 4th. Gospel, 3 Epistles
and Revelations

Jonson, Ben, 1572-1637, English dramatist, Poet Laureate 1619.

Jove, Chief Greek god.

Juno, Chief Roman goddess, Hera to the Greeks.

Jupiter, Chief Roman god.

Kipling, Rudyard, 1865-1936, British author, poet.

Kubla Kahn, in 1264 founded, ruled new capital of Peking, China.

Lewis, Merriwether, 1774-1809, U.S. soldier, explorer.

Lincoln, Abraham, 1809-65, 16th U.S. President.

Lind, Jenny, 1826-1887, Famous Swedish singer.

Linnaeus, Carl, 1707-78, Swedish botanist, explorer, taxonomist.

Lombards, German people who ruled a kingdom in Italy 568-774.

Longfellow, Henry Wadsworth, 1807-82, U.S. poet.

Maeterlinck, Maurice, 1862-1949, Belgian author.

Magellan, Ferdinand, 1480-1521, Portuguese discover of Tierra
del Fuego, Straits of Magellan, also sailed for Spain.

Magnus, Albertus, 1198-1282, Theologian, philosopher, natural
historian.

Mary Stuart 1542-87, Queen of Scots.

Melville, Herman, 1819-91, U.S. author.

Merlin, Wise enchanter in the Arthurian legends.

Miner, Jack, 1865-1944, Canadian naturalist.

Mohammed, c.570-632, Arab prophet of Islam.

Morgan le Fay, Enchantress of Arthurian legends.

Montezuma, 1480-1521, Aztec Emperor of Mexico.

Napoleon Bonaparte, 1769-1821, Emperor of France, exiled.

Nelson, Lord Horatio, 1758-1805, English admiral who defeated
    the French at Trafalgar.

Neptune, Roman god of the Seas, called Poseidon in Greece.

Odin, Ancient Norse god.

Omar Khayyam 1070-1123, poet, author of "The Rubaiyat".

Oswald, Saint, died 642, August 4th. is his saint's day.

Patrick, Saint, 389-461, Brought Christianity to Ireland and was
    said to have chased away all of the snakes!

Paul the Hermit, Saint, 4th. century.

Peter, Saint, his celebration day is June 29th.

Philip II of Spain, 1527-98, ruled 47 years.

Pliny the Elder, 23-79 A.D. Latin scholar.

Pliny the Younger, 61-105 A.D., Author.

Plutarch, c.46-120 A.D., Greek moralist, biographer.

Poe, Edgar Allen, 1809-49, American short story writer, poet,
    famed for "The Raven" 1845.

Polo, Marco, 1254-1324, Italian explorer of China.

Pompadour, Madame, Marquise Jeanne Antoinette Poisson,
    Mistress of French King Louis XVI, her favorite color was
    purple like the feathers of the Pompadour Cotinga.

Ptolemy I 367-283 B.C. 1st of dynasty of Macedonian Kings
    ruling Egypt 323-30 B.C.

Rodney, Admiral George Brydges, 1st. Baron, 1718-1792, Englishman who defeated the French Navy 1782.

Romulus & Remus, abandoned twins suckled by a wolf. Romulus killed Remus to become the legendary founder of Rome.

Roosevelt, Theodore, 1858-1919, 25th. President of U.S.

Rosselli, Cosmo di Lorenzo Philippi, 1439-1507, Italian painter.

Rossini, Gioacchino Antonio, 1782-1868., Italian composer.

Rothschild, Nathan Meyer, 1777-1836, Financier.

Scilly Isles, off the Southwest tip of England.

Scott, Sir Peter, 1910-89, Naturalist, sportsman, artist, son of Sir Robert Falcon Scott of Antarctic fame.

Shakespeare, William, 1564-1616, English playwright.

Sheba, Queen of Sheba, Ruled S.W. Arabia in 9th. century B.C. associated with King Solomon.

Shelley, Percy Byssche, 1792-1822, English poet.

Shogunate Days, 1192-1867, Hereditary military rulers of Japan.

Solomon, King, ruled 1015-975 B.C., Last son of King David, famous for his wisdom and power.

Stephen, Saint, Honored Dec. 26th.

Sullivan, William S., 1842-1900, Composer of Gilbert & Sullivan operettas.

Tennyson, Alfred Lord, 1809-92, English poet.

Thoreau, Henry David, 1817-62, U.S. nature writer, "Walden".

Tiepolo, Giovanni Battista, 1696-1770, Italian painter.

Turner, William, 1508-58, English writer, Father of British Botany, a minister who wrote on the birds of Aristotle & Pliny.

Valerus, Maximus, 1st. century A.D., Roman champion.

Vincent, Saint, died 1304.

Vinci, Leonardo da, 1452-1519, famous Italian painter, sculptor.

Wagner, Richard, 1813-83, German opera composer.

Wallace, Alfred Russell, 1823-1913, British author, zoologist, Father of Zoogeography.

Washington, General George, 1732-99, 1st. U.S. President.

Watts, Issac, 1674-1748, Non-conformist British minister, founder of hymnology.

Wilder, Thorton, 1912-83, U.S. author.

William the Conqueror, 1027-87, English King who defeated Harold at the Battle of Hastings.

Williams, Roger, 1603-83, U.S. clergyman founded Providence, Rhode Island.

Wilson, Alexander, 1766-1813, Scottish/U.S. naturalist, author, painter.

Winthrop, Governor John, 1588-1649, Established Mass. Bay Colony 1630.

Wordsworth, William, 1770-1850, English poet.

Zoroaster, born c.628, Author of the concept of good and evil forces.

Native Peoples Mentioned in Text

North America

Algonquin
Apache
Biloxi
Cherokee
Chippewa
Chitimache
Cree
Creek
Crow
Dakota
Delaware
Haida
Hidatsa
Hopewell
Huron
Iroquois
Kiowa
Kwakiult
Luiseno
Menominee
Mimac
Miwok
Natchez
Neskapi
Nookta
Ojibwa
Omaha
Paiute
Palute
Passamaquody
Pawnee
Penobscot
Plains
Pueblo
Seminole
Seneca
Seri
Sioux
Tlingit
Tsimish
Winnebago
Witchita
Yocut
Zuni

Mexican, Central and South America

Arawak
Atute
Aztec
Inca
Javante
Mayan
Olmec
Shavant
Tlascala
Toltec
Tupi